SIMPLY
ELEGANT
SOUP

SIMPLY ELEGANT SOUP

George Morrone

with John Harrisson   Photography by Joyce Oudkerk Pool

Ten Speed Press
Berkeley/Toronto

Ten Speed Press
Box 7123
Berkeley, California 94707
www.tenspeed.com

Distributed in Australia by Simon and Schuster Australia, in Canada
by Ten Speed Press Canada, in New Zealand by Southern Publishers Group,
in South Africa by Real Books, and in the United Kingdom and Europe
by Airlift Book Company.

Cover and text design by Jeff Puda
Typesetting by Kristen Wurz
Photography by Joyce Oudkerk Pool
Photography assistance by Shana Lopes
Food styling by Karen Shinto and Steven Fretz,
 with assistance from Katie Christ and Elliot Johnson
Prop styling by Carol Hacker/Tableprop
Project management and editing by Windy Ferges

The recipe for Jean-Louis' Chestnut–Foie Gras Soup (page 93) is adapted
with permission from *Jean-Louis: Cooking with the Seasons*, by Fred J. Maroon
(Lickle Publishing, Inc., West Palm Beach, Florida: 1989).

Library of Congress Cataloging-in-Publication Data

Morrone, George.
 Simply elegant soup / George Morrone with John Harrisson.
   p. cm.
 ISBN 1-58008-484-2 (alk. paper)
 1. Soups. 2. Cookery, French. 3. Cookery, American—California style. I. Harrisson, John. II. Title.
 TX757.M69 2004
 641.8'13—dc22

                        2004011386

Printed in Korea
First printing, 2004

1 2 3 4 5 6 7 8 9 10—08 07 06 05 04

For JEAN-LOUIS PALLADIN

and JOHN KUTROVACZ

Dedication

Jean-Louis Palladin, who passed away in November 2001, was the culinary professional who most influenced my career. When I think of him, there is only one word that comes to my mind: passion. He worked, taught, lived, laughed, or, very occasionally, raged—all with the utmost passion. There was never a low, medium, or medium-high with Jean-Louis. Whether he was playing pool, chopping onions, whistling in the kitchen, making stock, or charming his customers, he always performed to the max. Early in my career, when I was a line cook at River Café in New York City, I would make regular pilgrimages to his restaurant in Washington, D.C. I had never been to France, but no matter; Jean Louis was my window on classical cooking. Subsequently, I was fortunate enough to travel the globe with Jean-Louis and work with him, side by side. He always pushed the envelope and brought out the best in me—or forced me to confront my demons. I learned so much about unfamiliar ingredients from him, as well as new techniques, and he taught me all about being a perfectionist—I think of those times spent with him as my true apprenticeship. Perhaps the highlight of my career was dining with him at Alain Ducasse's restaurant in France—it is a memory I will always treasure. Above all, his soups were inspirational to me, and I will miss him dearly.

John Kutrovacz was one of the earliest influences on my career and a true mentor. He took my awareness of food, instilled and nurtured by my family, and showed me how I might apply it toward a career. John owned a bakery next door to my family's dry-cleaning business, and when I was just a kid, he would let me mooch sweets from his store. Later, as a teenager, I worked for him on the night shift, making cookie dough, filling doughnuts, and greasing molds and pans. Later on, he showed me how to make Danish pastries, custards, and fillings. Eventually, I was making cakes there. John truly enjoyed his work, and that positive attitude rubbed off on my outlook toward the profession. It was John who encouraged me to go to cooking school, and he even gave me a slightly tattered brochure about the Culinary Institute of America, of which at that point, I had never heard. I decided to apply, and my career took off from there.

Jean-Louis and John both succeeded in achieving balance in their lives: They were aware of the rewards available in their shared profession, and they maintained a concerted focus to achieve those ends. At the same time, they both also realized how important it was to enjoy their work and to be happy in it, and for this simple lesson of paramount importance, I will always be in their debt.

Contents

THE SOUPS

Acknowledgments

I WOULD LIKE TO THANK JOSEPH HUMPHREY, my former chef de cuisine, for his role in helping develop and test many of the recipes in this book. Without his help and encouragement, this book would never have been possible. Having worked with Joey for several years, I am absolutely certain that his approach and professional commitment will lead him to an outstanding and successful role as an executive chef in the years ahead.

Thanks are also due to:

Elliot Johnson and Steven Fretz for their invaluable contributions in completing this book. After working with Elliot in the kitchen for a few months, I gave him the nickname "Sunshine" because it sums up his persona and work ethic. Elliot radiates a love of life and a knowledge of his profession. I value his kindness, stability, positive outlook, and quiet leadership more than he knows. Steven's passion and dedication to food has made him an integral part of my brigade, dating back to my tenure at Fifth Floor. His commitment, loyalty, and character also reassure me that the torch we are passing to the next generation of chefs is in good hands.

Stacey Morrone, for her early contributions and assistance with the recipe writing.

Phil Wood at Ten Speed Press, for his perseverance and faith in me.

Michael Mina and Bridget McGill, the two closest people in my life, for their support and wisdom.

My daughter, Sydney, the youngest gourmand I have ever known, for all the laughs she provides me when times are tough.

Mom, Dad, and Pete, for all those meals we shared and for instilling in me the meaning of family.

John Harrisson, my coauthor and agent, with whom I first discussed a cookbook project many years ago. I consider him another friend who has always believed in me. With his help, we have arrived here at last.

Finally, thanks to all my true friends (you know who you are!) in the culinary field who have always supported me through the ups and downs of my career.

Preface

ONE OF THE INSPIRATIONS THROUGHOUT MY CAREER has been the writings of Ferdinand Point, a renowned French chef who ran La Pyramide, in Vienne. That restaurant, which is still open, was considered one of the best in all of France during Point's tenure. Point, who died in 1955 at the age of 57, is the author of a cookbook, also called *La Pyramide*, and it is a book that is peppered with some profound words of wisdom. I would like to begin this book by sharing some of the thoughts of Ferdinand Point that have particularly struck a chord in me.

"Success is the sum of a lot of small things done well."

"There are many people who claim to be good cooks; just as there are many people who, after having repainted the garden gate, take themselves to be painters."

"As far as every cuisinier is concerned, one must read everything, see everything, hear everything, try everything, observe everything in order to retain, in the end, just a little bit."

"In all professions, without doubt, but certainly in cooking, one is a student all his life."

"The duty of a good cuisinier is to transmit to the generations who will replace him everything he has learned and experienced."

Introduction

WHEN I EXPLAIN TO PEOPLE that I am finally writing a book that everyone has been encouraging (and/or pestering) me to write for years, their eyes light up; they grin or smile and enthusiastically say, "Please tell me about it!" I usually hesitate and calmly explain that is called *Simply Elegant Soup*. The reaction is always the same: silence. I can tell they are trying to figure out if they heard me correctly. "Soup? Really, a soup book? Why soup?" Sometimes they'll add something along the lines of, "But you're an accomplished chef, you should be writing a book about your repertoire, your successes, and the recipes your patrons have come to love. Why soup?"

Well, I'll tell you why. I am 99 percent sure that I've never encountered an individual who doesn't enjoy, love, or crave soup. It's a rare diner who cannot recall a favorite soup or dwell on memories that a soup has provided. I'll go out on a limb here and tell you what I *really* think: In my opinion, everyone has a soup fetish, some bond with a particular type of soup that goes to the core of his or her being. Many individuals are conditioned to think of soup as mundane, but soup can be much more complex than first meets the eye. I have always enjoyed taking the opportunity, as a professional chef, to elevate the status of soup on my menus, so that they are just as interesting and appealing as the other first-course offerings—and maybe even more so.

Where do I begin to explain my fascination and love of simple, little-old soup? I suppose it boils down to childhood memories and the food philosophy I acquired later on. Both have played a significant role in my love affair (marriage might be a better word) with soup. Childhood memories play an important part in shaping our ideas of comfort food and giving us an affinity for dishes that stay with us forever.

I am first-generation American. My mother was born in Buenos Aires, Argentina, and my father comes from Naples in Italy. That is as good a food combination as . . . well,

World Cup soccer! Both heritages are full of passion, whether it's for life, family, or food. I admire my parents because they had to learn a whole new language before they could prosper and enjoy the American dream, the reason they had come to this country. The wonderful thing about the United States is that opportunities are abundant for immigrants from every corner of the earth, and success can be achieved by anyone with the drive and desire. My parents are proof of this.

An important family bond in both of my parents' cultures involves the dinner table. Intertwined with the chewing and savoring of flavors is communication—it may be passionate, loud, and chaotic, or it may be affectionate banter—but Latins know it as conversation. Both my parents love to cook and are great home chefs. When they are cooking, they are at peace and relaxed; working in the kitchen is a love and a way of life, not a chore or a challenge.

When I was growing up, everything we ate in our suburban home in Maywood, New Jersey, was made from scratch, including what we drank at the table. Even my parents' wine was homemade, in the garage (even if it wasn't going to win any awards). Some of the food we ate in the summer months came from our garden. New Jersey is the Garden State, and I will proudly defend the state's reputation by asserting that Jersey beefsteak tomatoes are the best in America, and our homegrown crop was no exception. My great-aunt, who was my surrogate grandmother because my real grandparents lived overseas, lived in southwestern New Jersey, where I would spend a lot of time during the summer, enjoying her garden, which contained different kinds of fruit trees and a wide range of vegetables. Helping in the garden and experiencing the growing cycle firsthand added to my enjoyment of, and connection with, the food she grew, and created strong early food memories for me.

Unlike most families in my neighborhood, who ate dinner at 5 or 6 P.M. with milk and white bread at the table, we never ate dinner until 8 P.M. Both of my parents worked from 7 A.M. until 6 P.M. every day in their family business—they still do—and cooking meals from scratch meant that we ate later than most. As both my parents worked in the kitchen, nibbling on cheese while they prepared the meal, they would tease each other and laugh about the day, even after working together for the previous eleven hours. Talk about a different era!

For my family, dinnertime was family time, when we could all be together and talk. It was understood that neither my brother nor I were ever to miss dinner. There was no television droning in the background, no answering machines or other distractions, just quality family time. My grade school friends loved to eat over at my house if they could stave off hunger for that long. For most of them, it presented a whole new world of food and flavors and dishes that were very different from standard American fare. Conversely, I remember running home one day to tell my mom about the cool dinner I had eaten at my friend's house that came served on a silver foil tray with little pockets that separated all the food groups and even contained dessert. My mother was silent at first, then asked me if I had enjoyed it. I replied that, yes, I had, and babbled on while she waited patiently. "Good," she replied, "Because that is the first and last TV dinner that you'll experience!"

Soup was a staple in our home during every season of the year. In Italian, soup is sometimes referred to as *una cucina di casa* ("a cuisine of the home"), a concept that underscores its comforting qualities, its one-pot, informal style, and the fact that, most of all, it usually tastes better the next day. Some examples from my childhood were *pasta e fagioli* (a pasta and bean soup), minestrone, bread soups, as well as chicken and saffron broth (sometimes with rice), my mom's version of clam chowder, and of course, her lentil soup (see page 27).

My philosophy when it comes to soups, as a professional chef, is "flavor first." Soups are usually inspired by circumstances and ingredient-led—that's just the way I work. For example, just recently I wanted to add a scallop soup to my repertoire, and an old scallop sauce recipe of mine came to mind, so I built on that. If I see a stack of celery root in the kitchen, it may provide me with the inspiration to create an unforgettable soup. If I'm heading south from San Francisco on the Pacific Coast Highway past Half Moon Bay in pumpkin season, my thoughts will turn to concocting a seasonal squash soup that's bursting with flavor.

Soups are a wonderfully versatile and adaptable course. They can be comforting and satisfying, but they can also be elegant and sophisticated. Of course, it's relatively easy to create something special with top-quality ingredients such as lobster, or foie gras, or wild mushrooms. But part of the enjoyable challenge for me as a chef is to elevate sometimes humble and mundane ingredients to a special level, allowing them center stage, right in the spotlight. There's nothing that pleases me more than taking broccoli, or cauliflower, or squash, and turning it into a dish that causes my guests to say, "Wow!" You'll find those recipes in this book too, and I hope you will experience that same feeling of making a soup that stands out from all other soups that your guests have ever tasted.

I like to feature a separate soup section on my restaurant menus, offering my latest selection of soups, some of which you can find in this book. These soups have earned quite a reputation: Typically, more than three-quarters of my restaurant guests order a soup as well as an appetizer and main course, and they've let me know that they find the soup course a bit special. Because of my reputation for soups, some aficionados will drop in straight after work for a quick "soup fix" to alleviate the commute home. Perhaps because of San Francisco's often foggy and rainy climate, some of my soups (such as my *vegetable potages en croûte*) have gained something approaching a local cult following. This response is particularly gratifying. Some of my soups that are more complex—because of either the ingredients, or preparation, or presentation—are just as stunning and flavorful as any other course.

Enjoy these recipes. Some of the soups that follow are pretty straightforward—for example, Betty's Lentil Soup (page 27), the Cream of Cauliflower (page 41), and the Roasted Eggplant Soup (page 81). Other recipes are more challenging and require several steps. At the same time, do not be intimidated—by all means experiment with ingredients and simplify where necessary, as suggested in the recipe sidebar notes. The beauty of soups is that they are versatile—they can be rustic or elegant and made for large or small gatherings. Most of all, soup is a comforting food, with satisfying flavors and textures. So don't stress yourself out, but choose recipes that match your skill level. And if nothing else, sit back, enjoy the photographs, and allow me to guide you through the process of preparing unforgettable soups.

INGREDIENTS AND EQUIPMENT

Below are brief notes about the ingredients and equipment I prefer and how they are to be prepared, unless noted otherwise in a recipe. Use this list as a guide for selecting ingredients before you create the soups.

All ingredients (except for eggs) are assumed to be of medium size, unless noted otherwise.

Eggs are large.

Onions are yellow.

Garlic is peeled.

Tomatoes are plum (Roma) tomatoes.

Herbs are fresh. Bay leaves are dried.

Butter is unsalted.

Bell peppers and chiles are seeded.

The cooking oil I use most often is grapeseed oil because of its neutral flavor, high smoking point, and low cholesterol level. Safflower oil or canola oil have similar properties and can be substituted. Occasionally, I use cold-pressed extra virgin olive oil for its flavor.

Zest of citrus fruit is the aromatic, outermost layer of skin; that is, it excludes the bitter white pith. Citrus zest can be removed with a zester, fine grater, vegetable peeler, or sharp knife.

All bowls and pans are nonreactive (ceramic, glass, or stainless steel). Avoid aluminum cookware.

Kitchen equipment is assumed to be medium size.

TERMS AND TECHNIQUES

The following terms are used throughout the book to describe methods and techniques.

DEGLAZE: Adding a liquid, such as water, wine, or stock, to a hot cooking pan and scraping the bottom with a spatula or wooden spoon to dislodge the browned bits of food stuck to the pan.

DICE: Cutting ingredients into neat ½-inch cubes (the size of dice). "Finely diced" refers to ¼-inch cubes, while "coarsely diced" refers to ¾-inch cubes. Larger cuts are considered "chopped"; smaller ones are referred to as "minced."

ICE BATH: A large bowl containing a mixture of water and ice (about half of each).

MINCE: Cutting food very finely and neatly. Minced ingredients are less coarsely cut than diced or chopped ones.

PUREE: When pureeing soups in a blender or food processor, expect to do so in batches, using some of the solids and some of the liquid each time. Don't overfill the blender, and take care because the contents will be hot. I recommend using a towel to cover the top of the blender while holding the lid down by hand to avoid messy accidents.

SWEAT: To sauté ingredients (such as onions and garlic) in a pan over medium or low heat so that they soften but do not brown.

WATER BATH: Also called a bain marie. A large, high-sided pan used for baking in the oven. Ramekins, molds, or bowls (or other cooking containers filled with ingredients) are placed in the pan, which is then usually filled with enough hot water to come about halfway up the sides the containers.

Vegetable Stock

This recipe is a great base for any soup that uses vegetable stock. It uses the traditional method of incorporating ingredients together and simmering for an extended amount of time. An alternate method, which produces an even more ultimate stock, is to juice the raw vegetables and then combine the juices with herbs, spices, and water. Simmer this mixture until it is as sharp and intense as you like. The vegetable juicing should only be done with a juicer; do not try it in a blender or a Cuisinart.

MAKES ABOUT 4 QUARTS

1 tablespoon grapeseed oil
3 yellow onions, chopped
3 carrots, peeled and chopped
3 ribs celery, chopped
2 medium leeks, green and white parts, chopped
1 pound button mushrooms, washed and cut into quarters
2 heads garlic, unpeeled, cut in half horizontally
3 plum tomatoes, cut into quarters
2 tablespoons black peppercorns
2 tablespoons coriander seeds
6 sprigs flat-leaf parsley
6 sprigs thyme
2 dried bay leaves
4 quarts water

HEAT THE OIL in a stockpot over medium heat. Add the onions, carrots, celery, leeks, and mushrooms and saute until the vegetables are lightly browned, about 6 to 8 minutes. Be careful not to burn the vegetables at all. Add the garlic and tomatoes and saute for 2 more minutes.

ADD THE PEPPERCORNS, coriander, parsley, thyme, bay leaves, and water. Bring to a boil, turn down the heat to low, and simmer for 1 hour. Skim the surface of the stock occasionally to remove fat and impurities.

REMOVE THE STOCK FROM THE HEAT and carefully pass through a fine-mesh strainer into a large bowl or clean saucepan, pressing down on the solids with a wooden spoon to extract as much of the liquid as possible. Discard the vegetables. Use immediately or let cool and keep refrigerated, covered, for up to 4 days. Alternatively, freeze for up to 3 months.

Chicken Stock

By all means use a good-quality store-bought stock if you are short of time, but it's always worth making your own if you can. You can freeze some of the extra stock in ice cube trays so you can use it later in small quantities, which can be very convenient. Roasting the chicken pieces and bones (at 375°F for 45 minutes) before making the stock will really intensify the flavors.

MAKES ABOUT 4 QUARTS

4 pounds chicken pieces
4 quarts cold water, or more as needed
2 large carrots, peeled and chopped
2 ribs celery, chopped
4 yellow onions, chopped
1 large leek (optional), green and white parts, chopped
1 head garlic, unpeeled, cut in half horizontally
3 tablespoons black peppercorns
1 tablespoon coriander seeds
1 teaspoon kosher salt
4 sprigs thyme
3 dried bay leaves

COMBINE THE CHICKEN PIECES in a stockpot with the water, adding more if needed to cover the chicken. Bring to a boil over medium-high heat and then turn down the heat to a simmer. Using a large ladle, carefully skim off any fat or impurities that rise to the surface. Add the remaining ingredients, making sure they remain covered with water; add more water if necessary. Return to a boil, turn down the heat to a simmer once more, and maintain a simmer for 3 to 4 hours; keep the stockpot uncovered. Continue to skim the surface of the stock occasionally to remove fat and impurities.

REMOVE THE STOCK FROM THE HEAT and carefully pass through a fine-mesh strainer into a large bowl or clean saucepan, pressing down on the solids with a wooden spoon to extract as much of the liquid as possible. Use immediately or let cool and keep refrigerated, covered, for up to 3 days. Alternatively, freeze for up to 3 months.

Beef Stock

I like to save beef scraps and bones in the freezer, stored in freezer bags, until I am ready to make a stock. Then I add enough store-bought bones and scraps to make this stock recipe.

MAKES ABOUT 4 QUARTS

5 pounds beef bones
1 pound beef scraps
1 yellow onion, chopped
2 ribs celery, chopped
1 large carrot, peeled and chopped
4 cloves garlic, crushed
1½ tablespoons black peppercorns
2 dried bay leaves
About 6 quarts cold water

PREHEAT THE OVEN TO 400°F. Combine the beef bones and beef scraps in a roasting pan and roast, stirring occasionally, for about 20 minutes, until dark brown. Add the onion, celery, carrot, and garlic and roast with the bones for another 10 minutes. Transfer the bones and vegetables to a large stockpot and add the peppercorns and bay leaves. Add enough cold water to cover the ingredients. Bring to a boil over medium-high heat, turn down the heat to low, and simmer for 6 to 8 hours; keep the stockpot uncovered.

REMOVE THE STOCK FROM THE HEAT and carefully pass through a fine-mesh strainer into a large bowl or clean saucepan, pressing down on the solids with a wooden spoon to extract as much of the liquid as possible. Use immediately or let cool and keep refrigerated, covered, for up to 3 days. Alternatively, freeze for up to 3 months.

The
Soups

Chilled Tricolor Heirloom Tomato Soup with Avocado-Tomato Parfait

If there's anything that comes close to challenging the quality and flavor of vine-ripened summer beefsteak tomatoes from my home state of New Jersey, it's the truly traditional heirloom tomatoes that date back several generations. Their diversity and long-established heritage make them worth tracking down——or growing yourself. Each variety has its own distinctive balance of flavor, sweetness, acidity, and robustness. My favorite varieties of heirloom tomatoes for this recipe are Brandywine (red), Golden Jubilee (yellow), and the striped Green Zebra (green). As with any good tomato soup, ripeness is the key to success. For a simpler recipe, use just one type of tomato, such as vine-ripened beefsteak.

Note that at least two, and preferably three, people are needed to properly plate this dish. The soup should be served chilled but not ice-cold, because that would detract from the flavors. If you prepare the soup ahead of time or let it sit overnight, the heat of the chiles will intensify. If this is a concern, add the chiles shortly before serving.

Many local farmers are now growing heirloom tomatoes, and Seed Saver's Exchange, a nonprofit group, has a good selection of seeds for home gardeners. They can be reached at 3094 North Winn Road, Decorah, IA 52101, or contacted by telephone at 563-382-5990.

SERVES 4

Tricolor Heirloom Tomato Soup
2 pounds red heirloom tomatoes, cored and roughly chopped
2 pounds yellow heirloom tomatoes, cored and roughly chopped
2 pounds green heirloom tomatoes, cored and roughly chopped
2 green jalapeños, seeded
Salt and cayenne pepper

Avocado-Tomato Parfait
1 large ripe avocado, cut in half and pit removed
Juice of ½ lime
Salt and cayenne pepper
2 large plum tomatoes, cored, seeded, and finely diced
½ large shallot, minced
1 tablespoon minced fresh cilantro leaves

Garnish
2 teaspoons seeded and finely minced green jalapeño (about 1 small chile)
2 teaspoons seeded and finely minced red jalapeño (about 1 small chile)
4 sprigs cilantro

TO PREPARE THE SOUP, puree each type of tomato separately, using a food mill or food processor. Strain each type with a medium-fine strainer into a separate non-reactive bowl, making sure there are no seeds. Juice the 2 green jalapeños either in a juicer or by pureeing in a food processor and passing through a fine-mesh strainer. Add the chile juice equally to each of the three soups, stir well, and season with salt and cayenne pepper. Transfer each soup to a pouring cup (or a container that is easy to pour from) and chill until serving. (The longer the soups sit before serving, the hotter the chile flavor will become.)

TO PREPARE THE PARFAIT, spoon the avocado flesh into a food processor. Add the lime juice, season with salt and cayenne pepper, and puree until smooth. Set aside. Combine the tomatoes and shallot in a mixing bowl. Add the cilantro and season with salt and cayenne pepper.

TO SERVE, place a lightly oiled, small round mold (about 1 inch high and 1½ inches in diameter) in the center of each chilled shallow soup bowl. Sprinkle ½ teaspoon of each of the finely minced red and green jalapeño garnishes in each soup bowl, around the outside of the mold. Spoon some of the diced tomato mixture into the bottom of each mold until it reaches halfway up. Then add a layer of the avocado mixture, running a knife over the top of the mold to smooth the surface. Carefully remove the mold. With the help of another person, simultaneously and carefully pour the three soups gently around the parfait in each bowl so there are three distinct sections of soup. Try to prevent the soups from merging into each other. Arrange the cilantro sprigs on top of the parfait.

Chilled Haas Avocado Soup
with Hawaiian Plantation Shrimp

This recipe evolved during my participation in the South Africa Wine and Food Festival, held in Cape Town. For one cooking demonstration, I was given a grab bag of ingredients featuring avocado and shrimp and asked to spontaneously create a dish. With this book in mind, I chose to make a chilled soup, rather than the more obvious choice of salad. It turned out to be a big hit, partly because, as it turns out, chilled soups are something of a rarity in that part of the world.

I prefer to use Hawaiian Plantation shrimp for this recipe. If you can not find this type of shrimp, substitute any type of jumbo shrimp or prawn.

You can use frozen cocktail shrimp or crabmeat instead of the jumbo shrimp if you wish. If you are using crabmeat, combine with some minced fresh herbs and minced red onion and add some of your favorite creamy dressing to bind the mixture together.

SERVES 4

2 large carrots, peeled and chopped
2 white onions, chopped
4 ribs celery, chopped
1 cup white wine
8 cups cold water
4 small plum tomatoes
4 ripe Haas avocados, halved and pitted
3 tablespoons freshly squeezed lime juice
Salt and cayenne pepper
1 tablespoon grapeseed or safflower oil
1 tablespoon unsalted butter
1 pound jumbo shrimp (about 12 shrimp), peeled, with heads and tails left on

4 sprigs cilantro, for garnish
Freshly ground black pepper

COMBINE THE CARROTS, ONIONS, AND CELERY in a stockpot. Add the wine and water and bring to a boil. Turn down the heat to low and simmer for 30 minutes. Strain the vegetable stock through a fine-mesh strainer into a bowl and chill in the refrigerator; discard the solids.

PREPARE AN ICE BATH in a large bowl. Bring a saucepan of salted water to a boil over high heat. Score the bottoms of the tomatoes with an "x" and blanch in the boiling water for about 10 seconds. Remove with a slotted spoon and transfer to the ice bath to stop the cooking process. Let cool and then remove the skins with the tip of a sharp knife. Hollow out the tomatoes to make "cups" and trim a thin slice off the bottom of each tomato so it will stand upright. Set aside.

SCOOP THE FLESH OUT of each avocado and combine in a food processor with the lime juice. Puree until smooth, then transfer to a large mixing bowl. Stir in the chilled vegetable stock, a little at a time, until the desired consistency of the soup is reached. It should be slightly thick and might not require all of the stock. Season with salt and cayenne pepper and keep refrigerated.

JUST BEFORE YOU ARE READY TO SERVE, heat the oil and butter in a sauté pan set over medium-high heat. When the butter begins to foam, add the shrimp and sauté for about 2 minutes on each side, until bright pink and cooked through.

TO SERVE, PLACE 1 TOMATO "CUP" in the center of each chilled soup bowl. Arrange 3 shrimp in each cup and ladle the soup around the tomato. Garnish with the cilantro and sprinkle the soup with the freshly ground black pepper.

Duet of Chilled Beet Soups with Gazpacho Salad Garnish

During the summer season I always like to offer a chilled soup or two on my menu. My preference is for savory soups rather than sweet fruit-based soups for the first course. This particular soup is a natural choice for me because beets are one of my favorite vegetables. I like to use them in soups because they are refreshing on the palate, with a wonderful natural sweetness; they also make a colorful presentation.

To intensify the color and flavors of each beet soup, add a little red wine vinegar to the red beet soup to finish, and juiced jalapeño chile to the yellow beets. To juice a jalapeño, use a juicer or puree in a food processor then strain through a fine-mesh strainer.

If you have leftover soup, add vinegar to taste to create a vinaigrette for salad, or use it as a puree to serve with any white fish.

SERVES 4

Beet Soups
8 ounces small red beets, unpeeled
2 tablespoons canola oil
Salt and freshly ground black pepper
8 ounces small yellow beets, unpeeled
8 cups vegetable stock (page 7)
2 teaspoons white wine vinegar or champagne vinegar
Salt and freshly ground black pepper

Gazpacho Salad Garnish
1 hothouse (English) cucumber
¼ cup minced red onion
¼ cup seeded and minced red bell pepper
1 teaspoon minced fresh cilantro
1 tablespoon extra virgin olive oil, plus 4 tablespoons for drizzling
Salt and freshly ground black pepper
4 sprigs cilantro
Freshly ground black pepper

PREHEAT THE OVEN TO 350°F. Place the red beets in a bowl and dress with 1 tablespoon of the canola oil. Season with salt and pepper, wrap the beets in a sheet of aluminum foil, and transfer to a baking sheet. Repeat for the yellow beets. Bake both packages in the oven for about 30 minutes, or until the beets are tender. When cool enough to handle, remove the beets from the foil, keeping the red and yellow beets separate. Peel and set aside.

PREPARE AN ICE BATH in a large bowl. Place each type of beet in a separate saucepan, add 4 cups vegetable stock to each pan, and bring to a boil. Immediately transfer each soup to a blender and puree until smooth. Strain each soup separately through a fine-mesh strainer into a separate mixing bowl. Transfer each bowl in turn to the ice bath. Let the soups cool, stirring frequently. Season each with 1 teaspoon vinegar, salt, and pepper, and transfer to the refrigerator to chill completely.

TO PREPARE THE GARNISH, cut 40 paper-thin circles from the cucumber and reserve; dice the remaining cucumber and place in a mixing bowl. Add the onion, bell pepper, cilantro, and olive oil to the bowl and season to taste with salt and pepper.

TO SERVE, place a metal ring mold (about 1½ inches in diameter) in the center of a chilled shallow soup bowl and line it with 10 of the cucumber slices. Fill the inside of the mold with the cucumber salad. Simultaneously and carefully pour about ½ cup of each soup into the bowl, trying to prevent the soups from merging into each other. Gently remove the ring mold and repeat the process for the remaining servings. Garnish each salad with a cilantro sprig, drizzle with olive oil, and sprinkle with freshly ground black pepper.

Chilled Watercress Soup with Fresh Goat Cheese

In spring and early summer, I enjoy taking the opportunity to feature watercress in a leading role rather than just as a garnish. Watercress is an underused ingredient, which is a shame because it has one of the most distinctive and exciting flavors of any leafy green, and its peppery quality is a real palate stimulator. In this recipe, which plays on the popularity of goat cheese salads, the cheese balances the sharpness of the watercress, making a very satisfying, complementary combination. Whenever I put this soup on the menu, it always turns out to be a best seller.

If you prefer, you can use a dollop of crème fraîche, mascarpone, or sour cream as a garnish instead of the goat cheese. Any of these choices will be more neutral in flavor, but they will add a similar creamy texture. You can also make this soup just with spinach.

SERVES 4

Goat Cheese Garnish
½ cup good-quality fresh goat cheese, such as Laura Chenel
2 tablespoons extra virgin olive oil

Watercress Soup
1 tablespoon unsalted butter
1 cup chopped white onion
1 tablespoon chopped garlic
4 cups vegetable stock (page 7)
¼ cup heavy cream
1 cup spinach leaves, washed and chopped
2 bunches watercress (about ½ pound each), leaves and tender stems only, washed and chopped, 4 sprigs reserved for garnish
Salt and cayenne pepper

Garnish
Freshly ground black pepper
8 strips lemon zest
4 tablespoons lemon oil or extra virgin olive oil

TO PREPARE THE GOAT CHEESE GARNISH, place the goat cheese in the bowl of an electric mixer fitted with a paddle attachment. Mix the cheese on low speed until it is smooth and fluffy. Add the olive oil and continue to mix until thoroughly incorporated. Transfer to a bowl and chill in the refrigerator.

PREPARE AN ICE BATH in a large bowl. To prepare the soup, melt the butter in a stockpot set over medium heat. Add the onion and garlic, and sweat until completely softened, about 10 minutes. Add the vegetable stock and cream, turn up the heat to medium-high, and bring to a boil. Add the spinach and watercress and cook just until wilted, about 1 minute. Immediately transfer the soup in batches to a blender and puree until smooth. Strain the soup through a fine-mesh strainer into a mixing bowl and transfer the bowl to the ice bath. Let the soup cool, stirring frequently. Season with salt and cayenne pepper and transfer to the refrigerator to chill completely.

TO SERVE, SCOOP 2 TABLESPOONS of the goat cheese mixture into the center of each chilled shallow soup bowl. Carefully pour the chilled soup around the cheese and garnish with the reserved watercress sprigs. Sprinkle each serving with the freshly ground black pepper, top with 2 strips of lemon zest, and drizzle with lemon oil.

Classic Vichyssoise with Potato Latkes and Caviar

If you'll allow me to get carried away for a moment, this classic, elegant soup is like a beautiful woman wearing a terrific dress and expensive accessories. (You can see I take my soups seriously!) Vichyssoise is the ultimate combination of potatoes and leeks, and it's never looked or tasted as good as it does here, with the caviar garnish. Because it must be prepared ahead of time and served chilled, it's an ideal soup for entertaining in the summertime.

Choose the caviar according to your budget. Sevruga is the most economical, while beluga would be the choice for high rollers. My preference is for osetra, which falls somewhere in the middle, and which gives good value for the money. If I have the choice between caviar from Iran or Russia, I opt for the former as I find the product slightly superior.

SERVES 4

Soup
1 tablespoon unsalted butter
½ yellow onion, diced
2 cloves garlic, minced
1 pound leeks, white and light green parts only, washed and chopped (about 3 cups)
1 large russet potato (about 1 pound), peeled and chopped
8 cups chicken stock (page 8)
2 cups heavy cream
Salt and cayenne pepper

Onion Mascarpone
1 teaspoon unsalted butter
¼ cup minced red onion
¼ cup chopped yellow onion
¼ cup good-quality mascarpone
2 tablespoons minced fresh chives
Zest of ½ lemon, minced
Salt and cayenne pepper

Latkes
1 small russet potato (about 5 or 6 ounces), peeled
1 tablespoon all-purpose flour
1 large egg plus 1 large egg white
½ tablespoon heavy cream, more as needed
2 tablespoons milk
2 tablespoons canola oil

Garnish
1 ounce caviar
12 fresh chive spears

TO PREPARE THE SOUP, melt the butter in a saucepan set over medium heat. Add the onion, garlic, and leeks, and sweat until softened, about 8 minutes. Add the potato and stock and bring to a boil. Turn down the heat to low and let simmer until the potato is completely tender, about 15 minutes. Add the cream, season with salt and cayenne pepper, and turn up the heat to high. Bring to a boil and then immediately remove the pan from the heat. Transfer to a blender or food processor in batches and puree until smooth. Transfer to a mixing bowl and let chill in the refrigerator.

TO PREPARE THE ONION MASCARPONE, melt the butter in a saucepan set over low heat. Add the minced red onion and sweat for about 5 minutes, until translucent. Let cool and reserve. Pass the chopped white onion through a juice extractor and carefully fold the onion juice into the mascarpone. Add the cooked red onion, chives, and lemon zest. Season with salt and cayenne pepper, and chill in the refrigerator.

TO PREPARE THE LATKES, place the potato in a saucepan of salted water, bring to a boil, and cook until tender, about 15 minutes. Drain off the water and puree the potato in a hand-held food mill or mash by hand. Pass the potato through a fine-mesh strainer to remove all the lumps and transfer to a mixing bowl. With a wooden spoon, stir in the flour, then the egg, then the egg white, and finally, the cream and milk. The batter should be the consistency of a thick pastry cream; add a little more cream if the batter is too thick. To cook the latkes, heat the canola oil in a large nonstick sauté pan set over medium-high heat. When hot, spoon in the batter, forming 4 small cakes about 1½ inches in diameter. Cook for about 2 minutes, until golden brown on the first side, and then flip over and cook on the other side. Drain the cooked latkes on paper towels.

TO SERVE, POUR THE SOUP into 4 chilled shallow soup bowls. Place a potato latke in the center of each bowl. Top each latke with a spoonful of the onion mascarpone and then some caviar. Gently rest 3 chive spears against the latke.

Betty's Lentil Soup

Betty—my mom—instilled in me a love of cooking, and this soup of hers brings back memories of fall and winter meals, and of growing up in New Jersey. She would return from work at six in the evening and start preparing the family meal from scratch; we were used to eating late. What makes this dish really stand out in my mind is that it's one of my mom's rare vegetarian recipes—she's from Argentina, after all, where meat is served for practically every meal.

Since this soup is not pureed, take care to finely and neatly dice the vegetables as this will add to the visual presentation. You can experiment by making this soup with red or brown lentils.

For a more sophisticated presentation, serve the soup with a Parmesan tuile (see the French Onion Soup recipe on page 35, and use Parmesan instead of Gruyère). Shape the warm tuiles into baskets, using the back of a ladle, and fill with tender frisée greens lightly dressed with olive oil, red wine vinegar, and toasted pine nuts. The subtle bitterness of the greens, the sharpness of the cheese, and the pine nuts make an exciting counterpoint to the flavors of the soup.

SERVES 4

1¼ cups green lentils
2 tablespoons extra virgin olive oil
1 yellow onion, finely diced
1 large clove garlic, minced
2 ribs celery, peeled and finely diced
3 carrots, peeled
3 sprigs thyme, plus 2 sprigs for garnish
4 sprigs flat-leaf parsley
1 dried bay leaf
⅛ teaspoon cayenne pepper, or to taste
Salt
4 cups chicken stock (page 8) or vegetable stock (page 7)

COVER THE LENTILS with lukewarm water in a mixing bowl and soak for 20 minutes.

HEAT THE OLIVE OIL in a large saucepan over medium heat and add the onion, garlic, and celery. Sweat the vegetables for about 8 minutes, until translucent, making sure they do not brown. Finely dice half of the carrots and grate the remaining half; add both to the pan along with the thyme, parsley, the bay leaf, cayenne pepper, and salt.

DRAIN AND RINSE THE LENTILS and add them to the pan. Add the stock, bring to a simmer, and skim off any foam or impurities that rise to the surface. Cover the pan, turn down the heat to low, and cook for 45 to 60 minutes, until the lentils are tender. Remove the thyme, parsley, and bay leaf and adjust the seasonings.

FINELY MINCE THE REMAINING 2 THYME SPRIGS. To serve, ladle the soup into warm shallow soup bowls and sprinkle with the thyme.

Oyster Bisque with Leek Flan

The challenge of this recipe is to surpass the distinctive flavor of a perfect raw oyster, and I am proud of the results. This is a regal soup, and not just because it contains Champagne and just enough cream: it is silky, sexy, light in texture, and pristine in flavor. It is all-important to know the source, and therefore the freshness, of your oysters—those living near the ocean should be at an advantage. Buying fresh shucked oysters will work, but canned or bottled oysters will not do you justice.

This recipe uses a total of 3 cups Champagne, so one bottle will suffice. Use meaty fresh oysters rather than a delicate variety for this recipe. I recommend Kumamoto, Hogg Island, or Fanny Bay oysters from the West Coast, or Malpeques from the East Coast.

You will have more flan mixture than you need to fill the ramekins, but it is not practical to make less. Freeze the rest for another time, or use it in a quiche batter.

SERVES 4

Saffron Oil
¼ cup grapeseed oil
1 teaspoon turmeric
1 teaspoon saffron threads

Leek Flans
1 leek (about 4 ounces), white part only, washed and chopped
½ cup heavy cream
½ cup milk
1 small egg plus 1 small egg yolk
Salt and cayenne pepper

Oyster Bisque
6 cups plus 2 tablespoons heavy cream
1 tablespoon grapeseed oil
1 yellow onion (about 6 ounces), sliced
16 large oysters, preferably Hogg Island, Fanny Bay, or Malpeque, shucked, liquor reserved
1 cup Champagne
Salt and cayenne pepper
2 shallots, peeled and sliced
1 teaspoon saffron threads

Fried Leeks
1 leek, white part only, washed and cut into 2-inch strips
3 cups grapeseed oil

Garnish
2 cups Champagne
8 small oysters, preferably Kumamoto, Hogg Island, Fanny Bay, or Malpeque, shucked
1 cup grapeseed oil
½ cup all-purpose flour
1 egg, whisked
1 cup panko
1 cup diced deseeded English cucumber
2 teaspoons freshly grated horseradish
4 tablespoons chopped chives
Freshly ground black pepper

TO PREPARE THE SAFFRON OIL, combine the oil, turmeric, and saffron threads in a small saucepan over medium heat. Whisk continuously for 5 minutes. Remove from heat and cool.

TO PREPARE THE LEEK FLANS, preheat the oven to 250°F. Bring a large saucepan of salted water to a boil and cook the leeks for about 5 minutes, until tender. Drain in a colander and set aside. Pour the cream and milk into a large, heavy-bottomed saucepan and bring just to a simmer over medium heat. Add the drained leeks, turn down the heat to low, and cook for 2 minutes longer, stirring occasionally. Remove the pan from the heat and transfer the mixture to a blender or food processor. Puree until smooth and then pass through a fine-mesh strainer into a mixing bowl. Lightly butter or spray 4 small (2-ounce or ¼-cup) ramekins with nonstick cooking spray. Combine the egg and yolk in a large mixing bowl and whisk thoroughly. Slowly add the pureed leek mixture while whisking constantly. Season with salt and cayenne pepper and once again pass the mixture through a fine-mesh strainer into a clean bowl. Fill the prepared ramekins three-quarters full with the strained cream mixture. Place the ramekins in a shallow baking pan. You can discard any extra mixture. Pour enough hot water into the baking pan to come halfway up the sides of the ramekins. Cover the water bath with a double layer of plastic wrap. Bake for 30 to 45 minutes, until the flans are set and begin to pull away from the sides of the ramekins. Remove the flans from the oven and keep warm by letting them sit in the hot water until you are ready to serve.

TO PREPARE THE BISQUE, pour the 6 cups cream into a saucepan and bring to a boil over medium-high heat. Continue to boil, reducing the cream until 3 cups remain, 35 to 40 minutes. Heat the oil in a separate saucepan set over medium heat and sweat the onion for 5 minutes. Add the oysters and their liquor to the onion, continuing to cook over medium heat for about 3 minutes, or until the oysters are plump. Add ½ cup of the Champagne and bring to a boil. Add the reduced cream, return to a boil, and season with salt and cayenne pepper. Strain the soup through a fine-mesh strainer into a mixing bowl, pressing down on the solids with a wooden spoon to extract as much liquid as possible.

COMBINE THE SHALLOTS, the remaining ½ cup Champagne, and the saffron in a small saucepan. Bring to a simmer over medium-high heat and reduce until all the liquid is evaporated, 8 to 10 minutes. Set aside.

TO PREPARE THE FRIED LEEKS, thinly slice the leek strips lengthwise. Bring 1 quart water to a boil in a saucepan. Add the leeks and blanch for 2 minutes, stirring continuously. Strain, and transfer the leeks to an ice bath. Remove the leeks from the ice bath (do not squeeze the water out) and transfer to paper towels. In a heavy-bottomed saucepan, over medium heat, heat the oil. When the oil is hot, add half the leeks and fry until they are stiff but not brown, about 3 minutes. Fry the remaining leeks and reserve on paper towels.

MEANWHILE, TO PREPARE THE GARNISH, bring the 2 cups Champagne to a simmer in a small saucepan. Add 4 oysters and poach for 1 to 2 minutes, until plump. Remove the oysters from the pan with a slotted spoon and transfer to a small bowl. Add a little of the cooking liquid and keep warm. Heat the oil in a saucepan over medium heat. Dip each of the remaining 4 oysters in flour, transfer to the beaten egg, then toss in panko until thoroughly coated. When the oil is hot, add the oysters and fry until golden brown, about 2 to 3 minutes.

POUR THE BISQUE AND SHALLOTS into a blender or food processor and puree. Pass through a fine-mesh strainer into a clean saucepan and bring to a boil over medium heat. Whisk the 2 tablespoons cream in a small bowl until soft peaks form. Whisk the cream into the bisque and immediately remove the pan from the heat.

TO SERVE, UNMOLD THE FLANS by carefully running a knife around the inside edge of each ramekin and gently inverting each flan into the center of a warm shallow soup bowl. Ladle the bisque around the flan. Sprinkle diced cucumber around the flan. Garnish each bowl with 1 poached oyster and 1 fried oyster, arranging them evenly around the flan. Sprinkle each serving with the freshly grated horseradish. Drizzle 1 tablespoon saffron oil over the poached oyster, and sprinkle with 1 tablespoon chives. Place fried leeks atop leek flan. Sprinkle soup with freshly ground pepper.

Modern French Onion Soup with Gruyère Tuiles

To me, French onion is the Mother of All Soups, and I don't know anyone who doesn't like this classic peasant fare. Unfortunately, too many versions are, in all honesty, what I'd describe as "gut bombs," and making a truly memorable French onion soup is a challenge. The key to this elegant soup is the classic beef stock and the intense, sweet flavor of the onions. The delicate Gruyère tuile, or wafer, is a playful twist that echoes the hardened crust of a crème brûlée—you have to crack through it to get to the good stuff beneath. Make this soup only when you have the time to prepare the stock at home—store-bought stock will give you only average results.

To create a more elegant soup, poach four ½-inch disks of bone marrow (available from a good butcher) in beef stock for 30 to 45 seconds, and arrange on top of watercress sprigs resting on top of the tuile. Sprinkle with freshly cracked black pepper and fine sea salt.

SERVES 4

Tuiles
12 ounces Gruyère cheese, coarsely grated

Soup
2 tablespoons grapeseed oil or butter
2 pounds sweet onions, such as Maui or Vidalia, thinly sliced
¼ cup plus 1 tablespoon sherry vinegar
8 cups beef stock (page 9)
Salt and cayenne pepper

Garnish
Freshly cracked black pepper
4 small bunches watercress

TO PREPARE THE TUILES, preheat the oven to 350°F. Line one or two cookie sheets with parchment paper. Sprinkle the cheese over the parchment paper in a single layer to form four thin rounds, each just slightly larger than the diameter of the rims of the shallow soup bowls you will be using. Bake the cheese rounds until the cheese is melted and slightly golden in color, about 14 minutes. Remove the tuiles from the oven and let them cool on the sheet. The tuiles will become crispy once they cool.

TO PREPARE THE SOUP, heat the oil in a large saucepan set over medium-low heat. Sauté the onions, stirring occasionally, until they begin to caramelize and turn dark golden brown in color, about 20 minutes. Add the ¼ cup sherry vinegar and deglaze the pan. Cook until the liquid is reduced by three-quarters and the mixture is almost dry. Add the stock and turn up the heat to medium-high. Bring just to a boil, then turn down the heat and simmer the soup for 15 minutes. Season with salt and cayenne pepper and add the 1 tablespoon sherry vinegar.

TO SERVE, LADLE THE SOUP into warm shallow soup bowls. Carefully rest each tuile over the rim of each soup bowl (the tuiles should not be touching the soup.) Sprinkle freshly cracked pepper diagonally across each tuile and top with a watercress bunch.

Curried Crab Bisque with Crispy Softshell Crabs

Many chefs get some of their best ideas while traveling, and this recipe was inspired by a working trip I made to Singapore with my chef de cuisine, Joseph Humphrey. I had been invited to cook for a few days as guest chef at the acclaimed Shangri-La Hotel, and after dinner service, Joe and I would head down to the open-air food stalls at Newton Circus to sample the local flavors. The choice of spicy crab dishes was amazing—we were in spicy crab heaven—and right there and then, I decided I had to add a curried crab soup to my repertoire as soon as I returned to California.

Softshell crab season peaks in May and June. At times of the year when fresh softshell crabs are not available, use Dungeness crab legs dipped in the tempura batter recipe. Alternatively, garnish the soup with crab cakes.

SERVES 4

Crab Bisque
1 Dungeness or blue crab, about 1 to 2 pounds
2 tablespoons grapeseed or safflower oil
½ cup peeled and diced carrot
½ cup diced white onion
½ cup sliced celery
3 cloves garlic, crushed
1 tablespoon tomato paste
1 cup brandy
3 quarts cold water
1 dried bay leaf
1½ tablespoons good-quality curry powder
2 tablespoons long-grain white rice
1 cup heavy cream
Salt and cayenne pepper

Softshell Crabs
2 cups all-purpose flour
2 tablespoons baking powder
2 tablespoons cornstarch
2½ cups ice water, more as needed
8 cups canola oil, for frying
2 softshell crabs (about 6 to 8 ounces each), cleaned and
  cut in half lengthwise
Salt

PREPARE AN ICE BATH in a large bowl. To prepare the bisque, pour about 8 to 10 cups of cold water (or enough to cover the crab) into a stockpot and bring to a boil. Add the crab and quickly blanch in the boiling water for 1 minute. Remove the crab and immediately plunge into the ice bath to stop the cooking process. With a heavy knife, roughly chop the crab into 6 or 8 pieces.

HEAT THE OIL in a large heavy-bottomed saucepan set over medium-high heat. When the oil is almost smoking, carefully add the crab pieces and sauté until the shells turn bright red, about 2 minutes. Add the carrot, onion, celery, and garlic, and continue to cook for about 8 to 10 minutes until the vegetables begin to soften. Add the tomato paste and stir to coat the vegetables and crab pieces. Carefully add the brandy so that it does not ignite, and bring to a boil. Continue to cook until half of the brandy has evaporated. Add the cold water and the bay leaf, and bring to a boil. Turn down the heat to medium-low and simmer gently for 30 minutes.

STRAIN THE CRAB STOCK through a medium-fine strainer into a clean saucepan, pressing down on the solids with a wooden spoon to extract as much liquid as possible. Add the curry powder, rice, and cream, and bring to a simmer over medium-high heat. Cook for about 20 minutes, until the rice is completely tender. Carefully transfer the hot bisque to a blender or food processor in batches and puree until smooth. Pass through a fine-mesh strainer into a clean saucepan and season with salt and cayenne pepper. Keep warm.

TO PREPARE THE BATTER, combine the flour, baking powder, and cornstarch in a mixing bowl. Adding a little of the iced water at a time, whisk the ingredients together until the mixture reaches the consistency of heavy cream (you may need a little more, or a little less, than the 2½ cups of iced water.) Take care not to overwhisk; leaving some lumps will result in a lighter batter. Heat the canola oil in a large, heavy saucepan set over high heat. Dredge the softshell crab halves in the batter until completely coated. When the oil reaches 375°F, carefully lower the crabs into the hot oil, using tongs, and fry until golden brown and crispy, 2 to 3 minutes. Again using tongs, remove the crabs from the oil and transfer to paper towels to drain. Season lightly with salt.

TO SERVE, LADLE THE BISQUE into warm shallow soup bowls. Place half of a softshell crab in the center of each bowl, cut-side down.

Cream of Cauliflower and Roquefort Soup

Cauliflower is another vegetable that is underrated and underused. That's probably because it is cousin to the humble cabbage, yet it makes an elegant and tasty soup. I like to think that in this simple recipe, I've dressed up the Cinderella cauliflower and sent her to the ball! The combination of vegetables and blue cheese echoes the partnership between broccoli and cheddar in the recipe on page 55, so you can choose between these soups according to your mood.

Roquefort is one of my favorite cheeses, and I think it's the most versatile of the blue-veined cheeses—I like to use it in salads and sauces and paired with steaks or rack of lamb, as well as in soups. For this recipe, you can use another firm blue cheese, such as Maytag Blue. Avoid the creamier blue cheeses here, such as Gorgonzola.

SERVES 4

Port Mascarpone
1 cup port
¼ cup minced shallots
½ cup fruity red wine
½ cup good-quality mascarpone
Salt

Soup
2 heads cauliflower, leaves and core removed
6 cups milk
Salt
¼ teaspoon cayenne pepper
2 ounces Roquefort or other good-quality blue cheese

Garnish
3 tablespoons minced fresh chives

TO PREPARE THE MASCARPONE, combine the port, shallots, and wine in a small saucepan and set over medium heat. Reduce the mixture until only about 1 tablespoon of liquid remains. Pour into a bowl, let cool to room temperature, and carefully fold into the mascarpone. Season to taste with salt and keep refrigerated.

SET ASIDE EIGHT CAULIFLOWER FLORETS for garnish. To prepare the soup, roughly chop the remaining cauliflower and cover with cold, salted water in a large saucepan. Bring to a boil over medium-high heat. Cook for 10 to 15 minutes, until the cauliflower is cooked through. Drain off the water and add the milk. Return the saucepan to the heat and bring to a boil. Season with salt and the cayenne pepper. Transfer the soup in batches to a blender or food processor. Add half of the Roquefort cheese and puree until smooth. Pass the soup through a medium-fine strainer into a clean saucepan and keep warm.

BRING 4 CUPS OF SALTED WATER to a boil in a small saucepan. Add the reserved cauliflower florets and blanch for 1 to 2 minutes, until tender; drain. To serve, place two cauliflower florets in the center of each warm soup bowl. Pour the soup around the florets. Top the florets with a large tablespoon of the port mascarpone. Finely chop the remaining Roquefort cheese and sprinkle over the top of the soup, topping it with the chives.

Green Asparagus Soup with Chèvre-Filled Squash Blossoms

I call this a "happy soup"—maybe it's the vivid green color, the bright flavors, and the promise of springtime that seem to put my restaurant guests in such a good mood. Or maybe it's just me—cooking with the first asparagus of the year always puts me in an upbeat frame of mind because it's a sure harbinger of the growing season and the bounty of spring and summer produce ahead. The chèvre-filled squash blossoms give the flavor of this soup a little edge— the sharpness of the goat cheese contrasts wonderfully with the herbal quality of the asparagus.

One option to consider is providing a lattice of blanched asparagus in the center of the bowl (before carefully pouring in the soup) to support the squash blossom garnish. This will prevent the blossoms from getting soggy or sinking to the bottom the bowl. Cut 8 jumbo asparagus spears in half lengthwise, blanch them in boiling salted water for 2 to 3 minutes, and arrange 4 halves in a stacked square, like overlapping Lincoln Logs, in the middle of each bowl.

If squash blossoms are not available, you can garnish the soup by making the profiteroles on page 55, and filling them with goat cheese instead of cheddar. Use a fresh, soft and creamy type of goat cheese for this recipe; I particularly like Laura Chenel's chèvre, produced in California's Sonoma Valley.

SERVES 4

Asparagus Soup
2 tablespoons unsalted butter
1 small yellow onion, diced
2 cloves garlic, thinly sliced
2 bunches green asparagus (about 1½ pounds), trimmed and roughly chopped
4 cups milk
⅛ teaspoon cayenne pepper, or to taste
½ bunch spinach (about 4 ounces), washed and trimmed
Salt
½ teaspoon freshly squeezed lemon juice
¼ cup heavy cream

Chèvre-Filled Squash Blossoms
2 ounces soft goat cheese
Zest of ½ lemon, minced
6 fresh basil leaves, finely chopped
6 fresh purple basil leaves (or 6 more green basil leaves), finely chopped
2 sprigs tarragon, finely chopped
4 fresh chives, sliced thinly
Salt and cayenne pepper
4 fresh squash blossoms, pistils removed and washed carefully

Tempura Batter
2 cups all-purpose flour
2 tablespoons baking powder
2 tablespoons cornstarch
2½ cups ice water, more as needed
2 cups canola oil, for frying

Garnish
24 strips orange zest

PREPARE AN ICE BATH in a large bowl. To prepare the soup, melt the butter in a saucepan set over medium heat. Add the onion and garlic, and sweat for about 5 minutes, until soft and translucent. Add the asparagus and cook until tender and bright green in color, 3 to 5 minutes. Add the milk and cayenne pepper, turn up the heat to medium-high, and bring to a simmer. Add the spinach and stir until it is wilted, 20 to 30 seconds. Remove the pan from the heat and immediately transfer the soup in batches to a blender or food processor. Puree until smooth and pass through a fine-mesh strainer into a mixing bowl. Season with salt and the lemon juice and place the bowl in the ice bath to allow the soup to cool quickly; stir frequently.

TO PREPARE THE CHÈVRE-FILLED SQUASH BLOSSOMS, combine the goat cheese, lemon zest, green and purple basil, tarragon, and chives in a mixing bowl. Season with salt and cayenne pepper and mix together until thoroughly combined. Carefully fill each squash blossom with 1 to 2 tablespoons of the goat cheese mixture.

TO PREPARE THE TEMPURA BATTER, combine the flour, baking powder, and cornstarch in a mixing bowl. Adding a little of the ice water at a time, whisk the ingredients together until the mixture reaches the consistency of heavy cream (you may need a little more, or a little less, than 2½ cups of ice water). Take care not to overwhisk; leaving some lumps will result in a lighter batter.

JUST BEFORE YOU ARE READY to serve the soup, heat the canola oil in a small, heavy-bottomed saucepan set over medium-high heat (there should be at least 1 inch of oil). Dip the stuffed squash blossoms in the batter, covering them completely. When the oil in the pan reaches 375°F, carefully add the blossoms and fry for 1 to 2 minutes on each side, until golden. Remove with a slotted spoon and drain on paper towels.

WARM THE SOUP just to a simmer. In a bowl, whisk the ¼ cup cream to soft peaks and then whisk the cream into the soup. Immediately remove the pan from the heat and carefully ladle into warm shallow soup bowls. Carefully place a fried squash blossom atop each bowl of soup. Garnish with 3 clusters of orange zest.

Cream of Parsnip and Pumpkin Soups with Parsnip Chips

This soup captures the essence of the fall season, when Halloween is upon us and pumpkins are everywhere. It is the time of year in the kitchen when root vegetables really come into their own, with their hearty flavors and textures. In this recipe, the velvety, silky quality of the pumpkin works particularly well with the subtle spiciness of the parsnips. Sugar pumpkins are usually smaller than regular pumpkins, with sweeter and more tender pulp.

You can use acorn or butternut squash instead of pumpkin, in which case the color and flavors will be a little different, but equally satisfying.

Pumpkin seed oil is available at specialty food stores (and Williams-Sonoma, for example), or you can substitute hazelnut oil.

SERVES 4

Pumpkin Soup
1 sugar pumpkin (about 5 pounds)
1 tablespoon grapeseed oil
Salt and cayenne pepper
1 tablespoon extra virgin olive oil
1 tablespoon unsalted butter
1 large white onion, diced
2 small cloves garlic, minced
5 cups chicken stock (page 8)
1/4 teaspoon cayenne pepper, more as needed
1 cup heavy cream
Salt

Parsnip Soup
2 1/2 tablespoons grapeseed oil
1 leek (about 8 ounces), white part only, washed and
  thinly sliced
1/2 yellow onion (about 4 ounces), thinly sliced
1/2 jalapeño, seeded and thinly sliced
4 parsnips (about 1 pound), peeled and sliced
10 ounces celery root (about 1/2 celery root), peeled and diced
4 cups chicken stock (page 8) or vegetable stock (page 7)
1/2 cup heavy cream
Zest of 1/2 lemon, minced
Salt and cayenne pepper

Parsnip Chips
2 cups canola or safflower oil, for frying
1 large parsnip (about 6 ounces), peeled and thinly sliced
  lengthwise
Salt and cayenne pepper

Garnish
2 tablespoons pumpkin seed oil
Pumpkin seeds reserved from pumpkin
4 sprigs watercress

PREHEAT THE OVEN TO 325°F. Cut the pumpkin in half vertically and scoop out the seeds and fibers; clean and reserve the seeds. Place the pumpkin in a roasting pan, drizzle the flesh with the grapeseed oil, and season with salt and cayenne pepper. Turn the pumpkin flesh-side down and roast for 45 to 60 minutes, until tender. Meanwhile, prepare the pumpkin seeds and parsnip soup.

PREPARE THE RESERVED PUMPKIN SEEDS by tossing them in a bowl with the 1 tablespoon extra virgin olive oil. Season with salt and cayenne pepper and evenly spread out the seeds on a cookie sheet. Roast, stirring occasionally, until crispy and golden brown, 10 to 15 minutes. Remove from the oven and let cool.

TO PREPARE THE PUMPKIN SOUP, melt the butter in a large saucepan set over medium heat. Add the onion and garlic and sweat for 8 to 10 minutes, until soft and translucent; do not let the mixture brown. Scoop out the flesh from the roasted pumpkin and add to the saucepan. Add 4 cups of the stock and the cayenne pepper, increase the heat to medium-high, and bring to a boil. Add the cream and return to a boil. Immediately remove the pan from the heat, transfer the mixture to a blender or food processor in batches, and puree until smooth. Pass the mixture through a medium-fine strainer into a clean saucepan. Adjust the consistency of the soup with the remaining 1 cup stock, as needed. Adjust the seasonings with salt and cayenne pepper and keep warm.

TO PREPARE THE PARSNIP SOUP, heat the oil in a large, heavy-bottomed saucepan set over medium heat. Add the leek, onion, and jalapeño and sweat for about 5 minutes, until translucent and soft; do not let the mixture brown. Add the parsnips and celery root and continue to cook for 5 minutes. Add 3½ cups of the stock to the pan and bring to a boil. Reduce the heat to medium-low and simmer, uncovered, for 20 minutes. Stir in the cream, remove the pan from the heat, and transfer to a blender or food processor in batches. Puree until smooth and pass through a medium-fine strainer into a clean saucepan. Adjust the consistency of the soup with the remaining ½ cup stock, as desired. Stir in the lemon zest and season with salt and cayenne pepper; keep warm.

TO PREPARE THE PARSNIP CHIPS, heat the canola oil to 375°F in a heavy-bottomed saucepan that will allow the parsnips to lie flat; the oil should be at least 1 inch deep. Add the sliced parsnip to the oil and fry until golden brown, about 3 minutes. Remove with tongs or a slotted spoon, drain on paper towels, and season with salt and cayenne pepper.

TO SERVE, simultaneously ladle the two soups into warm shallow soup bowls, taking care to prevent the soups from merging into each other. Drizzle each serving with ½ tablespoon of pumpkin seed oil and garnish with the parsnip chips, some of the roasted pumpkin seeds, and a sprig of watercress.

Sweet Corn and Jalapeño Soup en Croûte

One of my favorite summertime snack foods is blanched corn on the cob brushed with chile oil, rather than the more traditional butter. That hot and sweet combination inspired this soup. Serving soup en croûte in the classic French style—ladled into a cup or single-serving tureen and covered with a puff pastry crust—is one of my signature presentations. I like to prepare a seasonal trio of soups en croûte at my restaurant, in the form of three small tastings per serving; this one is my personal favorite.

Use Tabasco green pepper sauce (or another brand) instead of the fresh jalapeños if you do not own a juice extractor. Alternatively, use a fiery habanero sauce, or use fresh green Thai or serrano chiles.

SERVES 4

4 ears fresh yellow sweet corn, husked and silks removed
2 white onions
3 ribs celery, chopped
3 cloves garlic
5 quarts cold water, more as needed
1 tablespoon unsalted butter
1 cup dry vermouth
2 cups heavy cream
Salt and cayenne pepper
2 jalapeños
1 (12 by 12-inch) sheet puff pastry, thawed
1 large egg, whisked

STAND THE EARS OF CORN on end and cut the kernels from the cobs. Reserve the kernels, chop the cobs into several pieces, and place the cobs in a large saucepan. Chop one of the onions and add it to saucepan. Add the celery and garlic, and cover the vegetables with cold water (add at least 3 quarts). Bring to a boil over high heat, then turn down the heat to a simmer and cook for 30 minutes. Remove the pan from the heat and strain off the cooking liquid. Reserve this corn stock and discard the solids.

MELT THE BUTTER in an 8-quart stockpot set over medium heat. Finely dice the remaining onion, add to the pan, and sauté for about 5 minutes, until translucent. Add the reserved corn kernels and sauté for 5 minutes, until softened. Add the vermouth and cook for 8 to 10 minutes, until the liquid has almost evaporated. Add 2 quarts of the strained corn stock and bring to a boil. Add the cream and return to a boil. Remove the saucepan from the heat and season lightly with salt and cayenne pepper. Transfer to a blender in batches and puree until smooth. Strain through a fine mesh strainer into a bowl and adjust the seasonings. Using a juice extractor, juice the jalapeños and add the juice to the soup to taste. Let the soup cool to room temperature (if you are not serving it immediately, store in an airtight container in the refrigerator and bring to room temperature before finishing).

PREHEAT THE OVEN TO 425°F. Ladle the soup into four ovenproof soup cups. Cut four rounds from the sheet of puff pastry large enough to cover the top of the soup cups. Top each soup cup with the puff pastry, seal the pastry to ½ inch below the rim of the cup, pinching by hand to make sure the edges are sealed. Brush the puff pastry with the beaten egg. Bake for 8 to 10 minutes, or until the puff pastry is golden brown. Serve immediately.

Cream of Broccoli Soup
with Cheddar Cheese Profiteroles

This all-American soup is a great way to get kids to eat broccoli—after all, who can resist the lure of profiteroles, even if they turn out to be savory rather than sweet? They make a fun presentation, and you can experiment with other types of cheese filling—Fontina, Gruyère, and blue-veined cheese all make good alternatives. The profiteroles in this recipe were the brainchild of Joseph Humphrey, my chef de cuisine for several years. They can be omitted if you prefer to simplify this soup.

Although I am not as fanatical on the subject as some, I do encourage people to buy organic produce when it's practical and cost-effective to do so. Organically produced broccoli is one vegetable that is pretty easy to find and is usually reasonably priced.

By all means use domestic cheddar if English farmhouse cheddar is unavailable. I do recommend a sharp cheddar because its flavor will stand out better than a mild cheddar and give more contrast to the soup.

SERVES 4

Profiteroles

½ cup milk

½ cup water

1 tablespoon unsalted butter

2 teaspoons salt

3 tablespoons all-purpose flour

2 large eggs

Profiterole Cheese Filling

¼ cup unsalted butter

¼ cup all-purpose flour

1 cup milk

½ cup grated cheddar cheese (preferably an aged English farmhouse cheddar)

Salt and cayenne pepper

Soup

2 tablespoons unsalted butter

1 small yellow onion (about 6 ounces), diced

2 cloves garlic, minced

4 cups milk

2 heads organic broccoli (about 1 pound), roughly chopped into 1-inch pieces, 12 florets reserved for garnish

¼ bunch spinach (about 2 ounces), washed

¼ teaspoon cayenne pepper, or to taste

Salt

Garnish

4 thin 2-inch shavings cheddar cheese

4 3-inch strips crisp bacon

TO PREPARE THE PROFITEROLES, preheat the oven to 400°F. Line a cookie sheet with parchment paper.

COMBINE THE MILK, WATER, AND BUTTER in a heavy-bottomed saucepan set over medium heat. Stir until the butter is melted, and then season with salt. Add the flour while stirring with a wooden spoon. When the mixture is combined and smooth, remove the pan from the heat. Add one of the eggs, stirring constantly; when the mixture begins to pull away from the sides of the pan, immediately spoon it into a pastry bag. Using a size 10 tip, pipe the mixture, about 2 tablespoons at a time, onto the prepared cookie sheet. You should have enough to squeeze out four profiteroles. Beat the remaining egg in a bowl and brush the profiteroles with the egg wash. Bake for about 15 minutes, until the profiteroles have risen and are golden brown in color; they should appear dry in texture. Leave the profiteroles on the sheet after removing it from the oven.

TO PREPARE THE PROFITEROLE FILLING, melt the butter in a heavy-bottomed saucepan set over low heat. Add the flour, stirring constantly with a wooden spoon until no lumps remain and the mixture is smooth. Cook for 5 to 7 minutes, until the mixture has a nutty, toasted aroma. In a small, heavy-bottomed saucepan set over medium-high heat, warm the milk until almost boiling. Slowly add the milk to the flour mixture, 1 tablespoon at a time, stirring constantly, until the mixture begins to thicken. Cook for 10 to 15 minutes or until the flavor of the "raw" flour is no longer apparent and the sauce is thick. Gradually whisk in the cheese and season with salt and cayenne pepper. Keep warm until you are ready to serve.

TO PREPARE THE SOUP, melt the butter in a large saucepan set over medium heat. Add the onion and garlic and sweat for 5 minutes, until translucent and soft. Add the milk and bring to simmer. Add the chopped broccoli (reserving the florets) and cook until tender, about 10 minutes.

MEANWHILE, PREPARE AN ICE BATH in a large bowl. Bring a saucepan of salted water to a boil and blanch the 12 reserved broccoli florets for 1 to 2 minutes, until tender. Remove the florets with a slotted spoon and plunge into the ice bath to stop the cooking process. Drain and reserve.

TO FINISH, ADD THE SPINACH to the soup and stir for about 2 minutes, until wilted. Season with the salt and cayenne pepper, transfer to a food processor or blender in batches, and puree until smooth. Pass the soup through a fine-mesh strainer into a clean saucepan. Adjust the seasonings and keep warm.

TO SERVE, bring a small saucepan of water to a boil and quickly reheat the broccoli florets in the boiling water. Drain, and place three florets in the center of each warm shallow soup bowl. To fill the profiteroles, place the filling in a pastry bag with a medium-sized round tip. Poke a small hole in the top of each profiterole and fill until slightly overflowing. Place a profiterole on top of the broccoli florets in each bowl. Ladle the warm soup into the bowls around the broccoli florets and profiteroles. Top each profiterole with more of the cheese filling and garnish with a cheese shaving and a strip of bacon.

Trio of Mushroom Soups

They say that necessity is the mother of invention, and that's true in the case of this recipe. I created this soup one fall when I had three different types of mushrooms sitting in the kitchen, and I just could not decide which type to use. I ended up using all three in the same dish, and the different flavors, textures, and colors make for a real treat. In this recipe, the nutty-flavored chanterelles contrast with the earthy portobellos and the more delicate lobster mushrooms.

The types of mushroom you use should depend on the season. In fall or winter, it's generally easier to find portobellos, porcini, and lobster mushrooms. In spring and summer, morels, chanterelles, trumpet mushrooms, and hedgehog mushrooms tend to be in greater supply. For a simpler soup, use just one or two types.

The white cipollini used here for the garnish have become more widely available over recent years. They are distinctive for their flattened, almost disklike shape. They are milder in flavor than onions or shallots, and they are softer in texture and more palatable when cooked.

Note that at least two, and preferably three, people are needed to properly plate this dish.

SERVES 4

Portobello Soup
1 tablespoon unsalted butter
1/2 white onion (about 4 ounces), diced
2 cloves garlic, minced
3 portobello mushrooms (about 14 ounces), cleaned and chopped (about 4 cups)
Salt and cayenne pepper
1/2 cup white wine, preferably chardonnay
2 cups chicken stock (page 8)
1/4 cup heavy cream

Chanterelle Soup
1 tablespoon unsalted butter
1/2 white onion (about 4 ounces), diced
2 cloves garlic, minced
4 cups cleaned and chopped chanterelle mushrooms (about 14 ounces)
Salt and cayenne pepper
1/2 cup Madeira
2 cups chicken stock (page 8)
1/4 cup heavy cream

Roasted Onions
4 cipollini onions or shallots, unpeeled
1 tablespoon unsalted butter, diced
Salt and cayenne pepper

Lobster Mushroom Soup
1 tablespoon unsalted butter
1/2 white onion (about 4 ounces), diced
2 cloves garlic, minced
4 cups cleaned and chopped lobster mushrooms (about 14 ounces)
Salt and cayenne pepper
1/2 cup dry sherry
2 cups chicken stock (page 8)
1/4 cup heavy cream

Garnish
1 cup micro herbs

TO PREPARE THE PORTOBELLO SOUP, melt the butter in a saucepan set over medium heat and add the onion and garlic. Sweat for 4 to 5 minutes, until soft and translucent. Add the portobellos, season with salt and cayenne pepper, and continue cooking for 8 to 10 minutes, until the mushrooms are tender. Turn up the heat to medium-high, add the wine, and deglaze the pan. Cook for about 10 minutes longer, until the liquid is almost evaporated. Add the stock and bring to a boil. Add the cream and return to a boil. Immediately remove the pan from the heat and transfer the soup in batches to a blender or food processor. Puree until smooth and pass through a medium-fine strainer into a clean saucepan. Adjust the seasonings and set aside.

TO PREPARE THE CHANTERELLE SOUP, melt the butter in a saucepan set over medium heat and add the onion and garlic. Sweat for 4 to 5 minutes, until soft and translucent. Add the chanterelles, season with salt and cayenne pepper, and continue cooking for 8 to 10 minutes, until the mushrooms are tender. Turn up the heat to medium-high, add the Madeira, and deglaze the pan. Cook for about 10 minutes longer, until the liquid is almost evaporated. Add the stock and bring to a boil. Add the cream and return to a boil. Immediately remove the pan from the heat and transfer the soup in batches to a blender or food processor. Puree until smooth and pass through a medium-fine strainer into a separate clean saucepan. Adjust the seasonings and set aside.

PREHEAT THE OVEN TO 400°F. To prepare the roasted onions, place the onions in the middle of a large square of aluminum foil, add the butter, and sprinkle with salt and cayenne pepper. Fold up the foil to form a pouch and roast the onions in the oven for 15 to 18 minutes, until tender. Remove from the oven, and when cool enough to handle, carefully peel the onions halfway, starting from the root end, but leaving the peel attached at the bud end.

TO PREPARE THE LOBSTER MUSHROOM SOUP, melt the butter in a saucepan set over medium heat and add the onion and garlic. Sweat for 4 to 5 minutes, until soft and translucent. Add the lobster mushrooms, season with salt and cayenne pepper, and continue cooking for 8 to 10 minutes, until the mushrooms are tender. Turn up the heat to medium-high, add the sherry, and deglaze the pan. Cook for about 10 minutes longer, until the liquid is almost evaporated. Add the stock and bring to a boil. Add the cream and return to a boil. Immediately remove the pan from the heat and transfer the soup in batches to a blender or food processor. Puree until smooth and pass through a medium-fine strainer into another clean saucepan. Adjust the seasonings and set aside.

TO SERVE, HEAT THE THREE SOUPS until they are warm. Transfer the soups to separate pitchers for ease of pouring. With the help of another person, simultaneously and carefully pour the three soups into warm shallow soup bowls so there are 3 distinct sections of soup. Try to prevent the soups from merging into each other. Place a roasted onion in the center of each bowl and top it with micro herbs.

Sea of Cortez Scallop Bisque

I first tasted bay scallops from the Sea of Cortez while vacationing in Cabo San Lucas on Mexico's Baja California peninsula. I enjoyed them several ways, both raw (in ceviches) and cooked, and I was struck by the fact that they tasted just as succulent and sweet as Nantucket and other prime East Coast scallops. They are now readily available on the West Coast and in other markets, too. This recipe is inspired by an old sauce recipe of mine and by the salty, citrusy tones of ceviches that I enjoyed on that trip to Mexico.

Samphire, also known as salicornia, glasswort, or seabean, grows on both the East and West Coasts. Its crisp texture and salty flavor make it a great addition to this soup, as well as to salads. By all means use another fresh seaweed with good texture instead. Samphire can be found at gourmet or specialty food stores. For an optional presentation, garnish the soup with lightly sautéed bay scallops.

SERVES 4

3 tablespoons grapeseed oil
1 teaspoon minced garlic
½ cup minced white onion
12 ounces bay scallops (about 60 scallops)
½ cup dry vermouth
2 cups heavy cream
1 cup crème fraîche
Salt and cayenne pepper

4 fresh pink scallops, in the shell, for garnish (optional)
¼ cup fresh samphire, cut into 2-inch lengths, for garnish
4 peeled lemon segments, for garnish
Freshly cracked pink pepper, for garnish

HEAT 2 TABLESPOONS OF THE OIL in a saucepan set over medium heat. Add the garlic and onion and sweat until soft, about 8 minutes. Reserving 20 of the scallops (about one-third of the total) for the garnish, add the remaining two-thirds of the scallops to the pan and sauté for 3 or 4 minutes, taking care not to let the mixture caramelize. Add the vermouth and bring to a boil. Add the cream and crème fraîche, return to a boil, and season lightly with salt and cayenne pepper. Transfer to a blender, in batches if necessary, and puree until smooth. Strain through a fine-mesh strainer into a clean saucepan and keep warm.

HEAT THE REMAINING 1 TABLESPOON oil in a large sauté pan set over medium heat. When the oil is hot and almost smoking, carefully add the 20 remaining bay scallops and sauté for 5 to 6 minutes, until well caramelized. Remove the scallops with a slotted spoon and transfer them to a small mixing bowl. Add the pink scallops to the pan, cover, and sauté for 4 to 5 minutes, shaking the pan frequently, just until they open. Set aside on a plate.

BRING A SMALL SAUCEPAN OF WATER to a boil and add the samphire. Blanch for 30 seconds, drain, and add to the bowl containing the 20 cooked scallops. Season with salt and cayenne pepper. Divide the mixture among four warm wide soup bowls, arranging it in the center, and ladle the warm soup around. Garnish each serving by placing a cooked pink scallop and a lemon segment on top of the cooked scallops in the center of each bowl and sprinkling with freshly cracked pepper.

Trio of Legume Soups with Smoked Ham Hock and Lentil Parfait

Bean and split pea soups are natural choices for the winter months; the ingredients are in season, they are real comfort foods that are best enjoyed during chilly weather, and above all, people love them. Sometimes it is hard to choose which ingredients in the legume family to use, so I decided to combine three of my favorites to maximize all options. The salty, smoky quality of the ham hocks really brings this dish together.

Note that the scarlet runner beans and lima beans need to soak overnight.

For the parfaits, you will need metal ring molds that are about 1 inch tall and 1½ inches in diameter. You can garnish the parfaits with fried herb leaves instead of micro greens if you prefer. Heat 1 cup of canola oil to 350°F in a sauté pan and add the leaves taken from the sprigs called for in the recipe. Fry until crisp and translucent, about 1 minute.

Note that at least two, and preferably three, people are needed to properly plate this dish.

SERVES 4

Split Pea Soup

1 pound ham hocks
4 ounces carrots, peeled and roughly chopped
4 ounces celery, roughly chopped
4 ounces yellow onion, roughly chopped
1 dried bay leaf
½ cup dried split peas, rinsed well and drained
Salt and cayenne pepper

Scarlet Runner Bean Soup

½ cup dried scarlet runner beans, soaked overnight in cold water and drained
4 cups chicken stock (page 8)
2 dried bay leaves
Salt and cayenne pepper

Peruvian Lima Bean Soup

½ cup dried Peruvian lima beans, cannellini beans, or white navy beans, soaked overnight in cold water and drained
4 cups chicken stock (page 8)
1 head garlic, cut in half horizontally
1 tablespoon grapeseed oil
Salt and cayenne pepper

Parfait

½ cup dried black beluga lentils, rinsed well and drained
2 tablespoons minced shallots
1 tablespoon sherry vinegar
1 tablespoon extra virgin olive oil
1 teaspoon chopped fresh thyme leaves
Salt and cayenne pepper
4 slices pancetta (or smoked bacon), cut paper thin
2 cups canola oil
1 cup micro greens

TO PREPARE THE SPLIT PEA SOUP, combine the ham hocks, carrots, celery, onion, and bay leaf in a stockpot. Add just enough cold water to cover. Bring to a boil over high heat, turn down the heat to medium-low, and simmer for about 3 hours, until the ham hocks are very tender. Carefully strain the broth through a fine-mesh strainer and reserve; set the ham hocks aside and discard the vegetables. When the ham hocks are cool enough to handle, remove the meat from the bones and reserve for the parfait.

COMBINE THE SPLIT PEAS in a saucepan and with 4 cups of the ham hock broth (refrigerate or freeze any remaining broth for stock or another use). Bring the split peas to a boil over high heat, turn down the heat to low, and simmer for about 45 minutes, until tender. Transfer the split peas and broth to a blender or food processor in batches and puree until smooth. Return to a clean saucepan, season with salt and cayenne pepper, and set aside.

TO PREPARE THE RUNNER BEAN SOUP, combine the drained beans with the stock and bay leaves in a large saucepan. Bring to a boil over high heat, turn down the heat to low, and simmer for about 1 hour, until the beans are completely cooked through. Using tongs or a slotted spoon, carefully remove the bay leaves and discard. Transfer the beans and stock to a blender or food processor in batches and puree until smooth. Return to a clean saucepan, season with salt and cayenne pepper, and set aside.

TO PREPARE THE LIMA BEAN SOUP, combine the drained beans and stock in a large saucepan. Bring to a boil over high heat, turn down the heat to low, and simmer for about 1 hour, until the beans are completely cooked through. Meanwhile, preheat the oven to 400°F. Drizzle each half of the garlic head with the oil, wrap in foil, and roast until soft, about 25 minutes. Remove from the oven and, when cool enough to handle, unwrap the garlic. Squeeze the roasted garlic from each half into the beans.

Transfer the beans and stock to a blender or food processor in batches and puree until smooth. Return to a clean saucepan, season with salt and cayenne pepper, and set aside.

TO PREPARE THE PARFAIT, place the drained lentils in a large saucepan and add 4 cups of cold water. Bring to a boil over high heat, turn down the heat to low, and simmer for about 30 minutes, until the lentils are just cooked through. Drain the lentils and transfer to a mixing bowl. Add the shallots, vinegar, olive oil, and thyme. Mix together thoroughly and season with salt and cayenne pepper. Set aside at room temperature. Carefully wrap each pancetta slice around a 1½-inch metal ring mold (see sidebar), trim the bottoms so they are even, and secure with butcher's twine. In a saucepan just large enough to hold the ring molds in a single layer, heat the canola oil to 375°F (there should be at least 1 inch of oil). Carefully add the pancetta molds and fry until the pancetta becomes crispy and caramelized, about 5 minutes. Using tongs or a slotted spoon, carefully remove the molds from the oil and drain on several layers of paper towels. When cool enough to handle, remove the twine and slide the pancetta rings off the molds.

WHEN YOU ARE READY TO SERVE, warm each soup to just a simmer. Meanwhile, place a pancetta ring in the center of each warm shallow soup bowl. Fill with alternating layers of lentils and ham hock meat (use about 1 teaspoon for each layer and gently press down with the back of the spoon after adding each layer). Repeat for each pancetta ring. Garnish each parfait with micro greens.

WITH THE HELP OF ANOTHER PERSON, simultaneously and carefully pour about ¼ cup of each warm soup into each bowl so there are 3 distinct sections of soup. Try to prevent the soups from merging into each other.

Soupe de Poisson

The classic Mediterranean-style bouillabaisse is a hallmark of Provençal cooking. In my version, I have focused on intensifying the flavors that fish can provide, rather than including shellfish, as bouillabaisse does. For this reason, select the freshest fish you can find, and be sure to use a high-quality dry white wine, because these ingredients will make all the difference in the end result. You will enjoy the bright flavors that this dish has to offer.

Although snapper or rock cod are the fish of choice for this recipe, you can use any firm, white-fleshed fish, such as striped bass or sole.

If you have the time, consider serving the aioli on crostini. Cut four diagonal slices from a baguette loaf and brush with olive oil. Season with salt and pepper and toast in an oven at 350°F until golden brown. Let cool a little and then spread the aioli on the toasted bread. Serve with the soup.

Leftover aioli can be stored in the refrigerator for up to one week. Use it as an accompaniment for fish, or serve it as a dip for shrimp or vegetables.

SERVES 4

Soup

3 tablespoons grapeseed or safflower oil
3 pounds whole snapper or rock cod, chopped into 2-inch pieces
Salt and cayenne pepper
1 white onion, minced
4 cloves garlic, minced
2 ribs celery, minced
½ cup finely diced plum tomatoes with their juices
1 teaspoon saffron threads
1 dried bay leaf
1 cup white wine, preferably chardonnay
3 cups water
1 tablespoon freshly squeezed lemon juice
Zest of 1 lemon, grated
2 tablespoons chopped fresh flat-leaf parsley

Saffron-Garlic Aioli

3 cloves garlic
1 teaspoon saffron threads
2 large egg yolks
1 cup grapeseed or safflower oil
Salt

Fish Garnish

2 tablespoons grapeseed or safflower oil
8 ounces red snapper fillet, skin on, cut into eight 1-ounce pieces
Salt and cayenne pepper
4 sprigs flat-leaf parsley

TO PREPARE THE SOUP, heat the oil in a large saucepan set over medium-high heat until it is almost smoking. Season the fish generously with salt and cayenne pepper and carefully add to the pan. Sear in batches on all sides, about 2 to 3 minutes. Remove the fish pieces and set aside. Add the onion, garlic, and celery to the pan and sauté until the vegetables begin to soften, about 2 minutes. Return the fish pieces to the pan together with the tomatoes and their juice, the saffron, and bay leaf. Add the wine and bring to a boil. Add the water and return to a boil. Turn down the heat to medium-low, cover the pan, and simmer for 30 minutes.

MEANWHILE, PREPARE THE AIOLI. Combine the garlic and saffron in a food processor and process until a paste forms. Add the egg yolks and process until completely incorporated. While still processing, slowly add the oil until it is completely emulsified. Season with salt and keep refrigerated.

TRANSFER THE SOUP to a food mill and mill until only the fish bones remain. Pass the soup through a medium-fine mesh strainer into a clean saucepan, pressing down on the solids with a wooden spoon to extract as much of the liquid as possible. Season the soup with salt and cayenne pepper and stir in the lemon juice, lemon zest, and parsley. Keep warm.

FOR THE FISH GARNISH, heat the oil in a large sauté pan set over medium-high heat. Season the fish with salt and cayenne pepper. When the oil just begins to smoke, carefully add the fish, skin side down. Sauté for 1 to 2 minutes, until the skin becomes crispy. Turn the fillets over, remove the pan from the heat, and let the fillets finish cooking off the heat, about 1 minute longer.

TO SERVE, POUR THE SOUP into four warm deep soup bowls. Place two fish fillets in the center of each bowl and dollop about 1 tablespoon of the aioli on top of each fillet. Top with a parsley sprig.

Carrot-Ginger Soup
with Lime Crème Fraîche

I created this favorite back in the 1980s, when I was executive chef at the Hotel Bel-Air in Los Angeles. That was the first time I was in charge of my own kitchen, and this was a healthful dish for all the "beautiful people." It contains a classic combination of flavors, and the lime juice really brings all the other ingredients together. You could serve this as a cold soup in summertime, in which case I would recommend thinning the consistency a little with sparkling water or additional stock.

The ginger oil will keep indefinitely in the refrigerator; it makes a good drizzle for grilled fish and poultry, salads, or vegetables, such as asparagus. To dress up this soup even more, add some grated lime zest and blanched baby carrots as additional garnish.

If you prefer to make your own crème fraîche for this recipe rather than using store-bought, just mix 2 tablespoons of sour cream with 2 tablespoons of heavy cream. The lime crème fraîche may be stored in an airtight container in the refrigerator for up to 3 days.

SERVES 4

Ginger Oil
1 cup canola oil
2 tablespoons powdered ginger
1½ tablespoons ground turmeric

Carrot-Ginger Soup
2½ tablespoons olive oil
1 tablespoon ginger oil (above)
1 white onion, thinly sliced
1 small clove garlic, minced
1 small green jalapeño, seeded and thinly sliced
1 teaspoon peeled and grated fresh ginger
4 large carrots (about 1 pound), peeled and sliced
4 cups chicken stock (page 8) or vegetable stock (page 7)
Salt and cayenne pepper

Lime Crème Fraîche
¼ cup crème fraîche
Zest and juice of 1 lime
1 tablespoon minced fresh cilantro
Salt

Garnish
4 teaspoons ginger oil (above)
12 sprigs cilantro
Freshly cracked black pepper

TO PREPARE THE GINGER OIL, combine the canola oil, powdered ginger, and turmeric in a small nonreactive bowl. Carefully whisk together and pour into a small saucepan. Bring to a simmer over medium-high heat and then return to a clean nonreactive bowl. Refrigerate overnight. The following day, carefully ladle off the yellow ginger oil and store in a bottle or other airtight container; discard the solids. Keep refrigerated until needed.

FOR THE SOUP, pour the olive oil and 1 tablespoon of the ginger oil into a saucepan set over medium heat. Add the onion, garlic, jalapeño, and ginger, and sweat for about 5 minutes, until translucent; do not let brown. Add the carrots and cook for 5 minutes longer. Add 3 cups of the stock and simmer for 20 minutes, or until the carrots are tender. Transfer the soup to a blender or food processor in batches and puree until smooth. Pass through a fine-mesh strainer into a clean saucepan. Reheat the soup, adjusting the consistency with the remaining 1 cup of stock, as needed, and season with salt and cayenne pepper.

PUT THE CRÈME FRAÎCHE in a small bowl. Mince the lime zest and add to the bowl with the lime juice and cilantro; season to taste with salt. Whisk together until combined. Keep refrigerated.

TO SERVE, POUR THE SOUP into warm bowls and drizzle each serving with 1 teaspoon of the ginger oil. Diagonally drizzle lime crème fraîche (about 1 teaspoon per serving) across each bowl in the opposite direction. Place 3 cilantro sprigs across the top of the soup in each bowl, and sprinkle with freshly cracked pepper.

Cream of Artichoke Soup with Parmesan Flan

One of the great artichoke growing regions of the world lies to the south of San Francisco, around Castroville on the Monterey peninsula. It is less than an hour's drive away, and because of this convenient proximity to the Bay Area, I like to use artichokes when they are in season to make a wonderfully flavorful soup. Here, I have drawn on my Italian heritage to marry artichokes and Parmigiano-Reggiano cheese.

The inspiration for the flans comes from a Parmesan custard created by Suzanne Gershwin, the chef at Acquerello restaurant in San Francisco, whose creativity I greatly admire.

You will have more flan mixture than you need to fill the ramekins, but it is not practical to make less. Freeze the rest for another time, or use it in a quiche batter.

The plastic wrap used to cover the flans prevents a skin from forming on top. Plastic wrap does not melt in the oven at this temperature and does not affect the flavor of the flans.

SERVES 4

Parmesan Flans
½ cup heavy cream
½ cup milk
¼ cup grated Parmigiano-Reggiano cheese
1 large egg

Artichoke Soup
5 large artichokes (about 2 pounds)
1 tablespoon unsalted butter
1 cup chopped white onion
2 tablespoons chopped garlic
4 cups chicken stock (page 8)
1 cup heavy cream
Salt and cayenne pepper

Garnish
4 large shavings Parmigiano-Reggiano
4 sprigs watercress

PREHEAT THE OVEN TO 250°F. Lightly butter or spray 4 small (2-ounce or ¼-cup) ramekins with nonstick cooking spray. To prepare the flans, pour the cream and milk into a small saucepan and bring to a boil. Add the cheese and stir until melted. Whisk the egg in a mixing bowl and, while whisking vigorously, slowly add the hot liquid. Fill the prepared ramekins three-quarters full with the mixture. Place the ramekins in a shallow baking pan and add enough hot water to reach halfway up the sides of the ramekins. Cover the pan with a double layer of plastic wrap and bake for 25 to 30 minutes, or until the flans are set and begin to pull away from the sides of the ramekins. Remove the flans from the oven and keep warm by letting them sit in the hot water until you are ready to serve.

WHILE THE FLANS ARE BAKING, prepare the soup. Put the artichokes in a large saucepan and cover with cold salted water. Bring to a boil and then turn down the heat to medium. Simmer the artichokes for about 15 minutes, until tender and the leaves detach easily. Drain the artichokes and set aside until they are cool enough to handle. Remove the leaves and the fibrous center around the artichoke hearts, and discard. Set 2 of the artichokes hearts aside for garnish and chop the remaining 3 into large pieces.

MELT THE BUTTER IN A SAUCEPAN set over medium heat. Add the onion and garlic and sweat until well softened, 8 to 10 minutes. Add the chopped artichokes and cook for 3 minutes longer. Add the stock and cream and bring to a boil. Transfer the soup to a blender in batches and puree until smooth. Pass through a medium-fine strainer into a clean saucepan, season with salt and cayenne pepper, and keep warm.

TO SERVE, UNMOLD THE FLANS by carefully running a knife around the inside edge of each ramekin, and gently inverting each flan into the center of a warm shallow soup bowl. Gently ladle the soup around the flans. Slice the remaining artichokes into 8 wedges and place 2 wedges on top of each flan. Sprinkle the flans with the shaved cheese and garnish with the watercress.

New England–Style Five-Clam Chowder

Before you glance at this recipe and decide that finding five different types of clam is impractical, let me hasten to assure you that you can make a perfectly delicious chowder with just one type of clam. The more the merrier though, because different types of clam have different flavors, textures, and degrees of saltiness. This chowder is made in the New England style, which has a milk or cream base; Manhattan-style chowders have a tomato base.

Other types of clam you can substitute are cherrystone, quahog, razor, butter, or propeller clams. Discard any of the fresh (uncooked) clams that are open; clams with a strong odor or that are heavy (indicating that the shells contain sand) are likely to be dead and should also be discarded. Conversely, be sure to discard any clams that do not open after the cooking process.

SERVES 4

1 tablespoon grapeseed or canola oil

8 ounces bacon, diced

1 white onion, diced

1 clove garlic, minced

3 ribs celery, diced

1 pound Manila clams, scrubbed and washed

1 pound mahogany clams, scrubbed and washed

1 pound softshell clams, scrubbed and washed

1 pound littleneck clams, scrubbed and washed

1 pound cockles, scrubbed and washed

1 cup bottled clam juice

2 cups white wine, preferably chardonnay

1½ pounds red bliss (or other red-skinned) potatoes, diced

1 cup heavy cream

Salt and cayenne pepper

½ cup chopped fresh flat-leaf parsley

1 teaspoon chopped fresh thyme leaves

24 strips orange zest, for garnish
Freshly cracked pink peppercorns, for garnish

TO PREPARE THE CHOWDER, heat the oil in a large stockpot set over medium-high heat. When the oil just begins to smoke, add the bacon and sauté for 3 to 5 minutes, until it starts to caramelize. Add the onion, garlic, and celery and continue to cook until the vegetables begin to soften, about 2 minutes. Add all the clams and the cockles, the clam juice, and the wine, and cover the stockpot. Check the clams after 2 minutes and, using tongs, remove any clams that have opened and reserve on a platter. Cover with the lid again and let the remaining clams steam for 8 to 10 minutes, until all the clams have opened. Transfer all of the clams to a platter and cover them with foil to keep warm. Discard any clams that have not opened.

ADD THE POTATOES to the cooking liquid and cook over medium heat until they are just tender but still firm, 3 to 4 minutes. Add the cream and season with salt and cayenne pepper. Bring the soup to a boil and then add the reserved steamed clams, parsley, and thyme. Stir to combine. Divide the chowder among four warm soup bowls, and top the clams with orange zest and freshly cracked peppercorns.

Roasted Eggplant Soup with Toasted Cumin and Pickled Eggplant

It is probably because of my Italian and Argentinian heritage that eggplant is one of my favorite ingredients. I associate it most strongly with my mom's wonderful pickled eggplant salad, and I have adapted her recipe for the garnish here. Unfortunately, eggplant is regarded by many people as the pariah of the vegetable world; it certainly doesn't get the respect it deserves! This colorful soup is my attempt to redress the balance.

You need to allow at least one week for the eggplant to pickle, and preferably up to one month, so plan accordingly. Leftover pickled eggplant makes a zesty accompaniment to green salads. It can also be used as a spread or to top bruschetta.

Two ingredients that complement eggplant particularly well are cumin and garlic. Toasting the cumin brings out it full fragrance and range of flavor.

SERVES 4

Pickled Eggplant
2 cups cold water
1 cup distilled white vinegar
1 tablespoon salt
¼ teaspoon dried red pepper flakes
1 pound eggplant, peeled
4 garlic cloves, crushed
2 cups olive oil

Tomato Confit
4 plum tomatoes
1 cup extra virgin olive oil
1 dried bay leaf
4 sprigs thyme
4 sprigs sage

Eggplant Soup
4 eggplants, about 8 ounces each
2 heads garlic
2 tablespoons grapeseed oil
Salt and cayenne pepper
8 cups chicken stock (page 8)
Juice and minced zest of 2 lemons
2 teaspoons ground cumin

Garnish
Zest of 1 lemon, julienned,

TO PREPARE THE PICKLED EGGPLANT, combine the cold water in a small saucepan with the vinegar, salt, and pepper flakes, and bring to a boil. Meanwhile, cut the eggplant into long strips about 1 inch thick and put into a bowl. Pour the hot pickling liquid over the eggplant and let sit for 30 minutes or until cooled to room temperature. Drain the eggplant, pat dry, and transfer to a clean jar or airtight container. Add the garlic and enough olive oil to completely cover the eggplant. Place in the refrigerator and marinate for at least 1 week and up to 1 month.

PREPARE AN ICE BATH in a large bowl. To prepare the tomato confit, bring a saucepan of salted water to a boil over high heat. Score the bottoms of the tomatoes with an "x" and blanch in the boiling water for about 10 seconds. Remove with a slotted spoon and transfer to the ice bath to stop the cooking process. Let cool and then remove the skins with the tip of a sharp knife. Place the peeled tomatoes in a small saucepan and cover with the olive oil. Add the bay leaf, thyme, and sage, and cook over the lowest possible heat for about 15 minutes; the tomatoes will be soft enough to just hold their shape. Turn off the heat and let the tomatoes cool in the oil.

MEANWHILE, PREHEAT THE OVEN TO 375°F. To prepare the soup, wash the eggplants and stab them randomly in several places with a small paring knife. Separate individual cloves of garlic from the heads, peel, and place 1 clove of garlic in each cut. Drizzle the eggplants with the oil and season with salt and cayenne pepper. Place in a roasting pan and roast for 35 to 40 minutes, or until the eggplants are fully cooked through. Remove the eggplants and when they are cool enough to handle, cut them in half lengthwise. Remove the seeds and garlic cloves. Using a spoon, gently scrape out the flesh and transfer to a large saucepan. Add the stock, lemon juice, and the minced lemon zest, and season with salt and cayenne pepper. Bring to a boil over medium-high heat, and then turn down the heat to medium-low. Simmer for 15 minutes. Transfer to a blender or food processor in batches and puree until smooth. Pass the mixture through a fine-mesh strainer into a clean saucepan and adjust the seasonings. Place the cumin in a small sauté pan and set

over medium heat. Toast the cumin for about 1 minute, stirring frequently, until it becomes fragrant. Stir the toasted cumin into the soup.

TO SERVE, RETURN THE SOUP to a simmer. Place 1 cooked tomato in the center of each warm soup bowl. With a paring knife, cut a slit down the center of each tomato and stuff with 1 or 2 pieces of pickled eggplant. Pour the soup around each tomato, garnish with the julienned lemon zest, and drizzle about ½ teaspoon of the tomato confit oil around each bowl.

Duet of Cream of Celery Root and Lobster Bisque with Tarragon Flan

This recipe takes me back to my early cooking career. I remember learning in a class on Escoffier at culinary school that bisques were originally thickened with rice. And lobster bisque is one of the first classic soups you learn to make in a brigade-type kitchen; working your way up, you soon become the "lobster bisque boy," in charge of breaking down the leftover shells and assembling the ingredients for the soup. Sometimes, I still get flashbacks from those days! I love the flavor of celery root, also called celeriac. It has a simple sweetness that marries well with the more complex flavor of the lobster bisque. For simplicity, prepare the soups and serve without the flan. Alternatively, either soup makes a wonderful dish just on its own.

Keep the flans warm by letting them sit in the water bath after they have baked. If you are preparing them ahead of time, reheat in a water bath before serving. The plastic wrap used to cover the flans prevents a skin from forming on top. Plastic wrap does not melt in the oven at this temperature and does not affect the flavor of the flans.

If you are serving this soup on a special occasion involving a guest of honor, consider a more dramatic presentation. Reserve the lobster head with its antennae, brush it lightly with oil to create an attractive sheen, and place on top of the tarragon flan and fried tarragon leaves in the center of the bowl. Be sure the lobster's eyes are staring your guest in the face!

SERVES 4

Tarragon Flans
½ cup heavy cream
½ cup milk
1 bunch fresh tarragon (about 1 ounce), leaves only
2 tablespoons washed, stemmed, and chopped spinach leaves
2 large eggs
Salt and cayenne pepper

Cream of Celery Root
1 tablespoon unsalted butter
1½ pounds celery root, peeled and cut into large dice
½ leek, white part only, washed and sliced (about ½ cup)
2 cups chicken stock (page 8)
1 cup plus 2 tablespoons heavy cream
½ tablespoon freshly squeezed lemon juice
Salt and cayenne pepper

Lobster Bisque
1 live lobster, 1 to 1½ pounds
2 tablespoons grapeseed or canola oil
½ cup peeled and diced carrot
½ cup diced white onion
½ cup sliced celery
3 cloves garlic, crushed
1 tablespoon tomato paste
1 cup brandy
4 cups water
1 dried bay leaf
2 tablespoons long-grain rice
1 cup heavy cream
Salt and cayenne pepper

HEAT THE OVEN TO 250°F. Lightly butter or spray 4 small (2-ounce or ¼-cup) ramekins with nonstick cooking spray.

TO PREPARE THE FLANS, pour the cream and milk into a saucepan and bring to a simmer over medium heat. Add the tarragon and spinach and stir until wilted, about 10 seconds. Remove the pan from the heat and transfer the mixture to a blender or food processor. Puree until smooth, and pass the mixture through a medium-fine strainer into a mixing bowl. Thoroughly whisk the eggs in a separate mixing bowl. Slowly add the warm puree mixture to the eggs while whisking constantly. Season with salt and cayenne pepper and once again pass the mixture through a medium-fine strainer into a clean bowl. Fill the prepared ramekins three-quarters full with the strained cream mixture. Place the ramekins in a shallow baking pan. Pour enough hot water into the pan to come halfway up the sides of the ramekins. Cover the water bath with a double layer of plastic wrap. Bake for 30 to 45 minutes, or until the flans are set and begin to pull away from the sides of the ramekins. Remove the flans from the oven and keep warm by letting them sit in the hot water until you are ready to serve.

TO PREPARE THE CREAM OF CELERY ROOT, melt the butter in a saucepan set over medium heat. Add the celery root and leek, and sweat for about 5 minutes. Add the stock and bring to a boil. Turn down the heat to a simmer and continue to cook until the celery root is tender enough to puree, about 20 minutes. Add the cream, increase the heat to high, and bring to a boil. Immediately remove the pan from the heat and transfer the mixture in batches to a blender or food processor. Puree until smooth and pass through a medium-fine strainer into a clean saucepan. Season with the lemon juice, salt, and cayenne pepper. Keep the soup warm over low heat, covered, stirring occasionally until you are ready to serve.

PREPARE AN ICE BATH with enough water to cover the lobster. To prepare the lobster bisque, bring 8 to 10 cups of water to a boil in a large stockpot. Place the lobster in the boiling water and blanch for 20 seconds. Remove the lobster with tongs and immediately plunge into the ice bath to stop the cooking process. When the lobster is cool enough to handle, separate the tail, claws, and head. Using the back of a heavy knife, gently crack the shells of the tail and claws and reserve. Remove the gills from inside the head and discard; rinse the head to clean it.

HEAT THE OIL in a heavy-bottomed saucepan over medium-high heat. When almost smoking, carefully add the cracked lobster tail, claws, and head, and quickly sauté until the shells turn bright red, about 2 minutes. Add the carrot, onion, celery, and garlic, and continue to cook until the vegetables begin to soften, about 5 minutes. Add the tomato paste and stir to coat the vegetables and lobster. Carefully add the brandy so it does not ignite, and bring to a boil. Continue to cook until half the brandy has evaporated. Add the water and the bay leaf and bring to a boil. Turn down the heat to medium-low and simmer gently, uncovered, for 30 minutes. Strain the mixture through a medium strainer into a bowl, pressing down on the solids with a wooden spoon to extract as much liquid as possible. Then strain through a fine-mesh strainer into another bowl. Return the liquid to a clean saucepan and add the rice and cream. Bring to a simmer and cook until the rice is thoroughly cooked, 20 to 30 minutes. Carefully transfer the hot bisque to a blender or food processor in batches and puree until smooth. Pass through a fine-mesh strainer into a clean saucepan and season with salt and cayenne pepper.

TO SERVE, UNMOLD THE FLANS by carefully running a knife around the inside edge of each ramekin and gently inverting each flan into the center of a warm shallow soup bowl. For ease of pouring, transfer the two soups to separate pitchers and then simultaneously and carefully pour them around the flan, taking care to prevent the soups from merging into each other.

Cream of Garlic Soup
with Escargots

Cream of garlic is a classic soup in France, which is where I fell in love with it. Given the ever-growing popularity of garlic in the United States, I'm surprised that you don't find garlic soup more often on restaurant menus. That's probably because people are reluctant to try it because they think the flavor will be overpowering, but poaching garlic completely removes its pungency and instead gives it a particular sweetness. Whenever I think of garlic and France, I immediately think of snails, so I added escargots here, together with parsley, their usual garnish. To complete the presentation, I serve the escargots in puff pastry in the center of the soup. I recommend using canned escargots for their more familiar texture; most American palates find the crunchier fresh snails more challenging.

For a simpler soup, omit the puff pastry and simply arrange the escargots on top of the soup. Alternatively, you can substitute frogs' legs or sautéed or poached shelled shrimp for the escargots.

SERVES 4

Soup
2 cups garlic cloves (about 8 ounces)
8 cups chicken stock (page 8)
1 cup heavy cream
Salt and cayenne pepper

Escargots
1 (12 by 12-inch) sheet puff pastry, thawed
1 large egg, beaten
1 cup fresh flat-leaf parsley leaves
1 clove garlic
2 tablespoons extra virgin olive oil
1 tablespoon unsalted butter
20 canned precooked escargots, rinsed
Salt and cayenne pepper

Garnish
4 large sprigs flat-leaf parsley

TO PREPARE THE SOUP, place the garlic cloves in a saucepan and cover with cold water. Bring the water to a boil over medium-high heat. When the water comes to a boil, remove the pan from the heat and drain off the water. Cover the garlic with fresh cold water and bring to a boil again. Drain the water once more and then add the stock. Turn down the heat to medium and return the pan to the heat. Cook (but do not let boil) for 8 to 10 minutes, until the garlic is completely tender. Add the cream and season with salt and cayenne pepper. Turn up the heat to medium-high and bring the mixture to a boil. Immediately remove the pan from the heat and transfer the soup in batches to a blender or food processor. Puree until smooth, pass through a medium-fine strainer, and transfer to a clean saucepan. Cover the pan and keep warm.

PREHEAT THE OVEN TO 425°F. To prepare the escargots, cut out four rounds of puff pastry, using a 2-inch cookie cutter. With a slightly smaller cookie cutter, or using a sharp knife, carefully score a smaller circle inside the pastry circles, taking care to cut only halfway through the pastry. Transfer the pastry circles to a nonstick cookie sheet and brush the top of each with the beaten egg. Bake for 6 to 8 minutes, until the pastry circles rise and are golden brown and crispy. Remove from the oven and let cool. With a small, sharp knife, cut out the top of the puff pastry cylinders where they were scored and then carefully hollow out the cylinder, leaving a pastry base on the inside.

PREPARE AN ICE BATH in a large bowl. Bring a small saucepan of salted water to a boil and add the parsley leaves. Blanch for 5 seconds, drain, and transfer the parsley to the ice bath to stop the cooking process. Drain again. Combine the parsley and the garlic in a food processor or blender, add the olive oil, and puree until smooth. Set aside.

MELT THE BUTTER IN A SAUTÉ PAN set over medium-high heat. When it starts to foam, add the escargots and sauté for 3 to 4 minutes, until warmed through. Season with salt and cayenne pepper and add the reserved parsley puree. Remove the pan from the heat and stir to coat the escargots with the parsley sauce.

TO SERVE, PLACE A PASTRY CYLINDER in the center of each warm shallow soup bowl. Spoon 5 escargots and some sauce into each cylinder, partly cover with pastry top, and pour the soup around the cylinders. Garnish with a parsley sprig.

Jean-Louis' Chestnut–Foie Gras Soup

Jean-Louis Palladin is one of my culinary heroes, and he became one of my best friends; in fact, this book is dedicated to him. This version of his signature dish is my tribute to him. His Washington, D.C. restaurant—Jean-Louis at the Watergate—won national acclaim, and although he died in November 2001, he will remain in the hearts of his colleagues everywhere. When I first started cooking professionally in the early 1980s at the River Café in Brooklyn, New York, I'd save my paycheck for two months so I could take the train down to the capital and eat at Jean-Louis' restaurant. I loved his food that much. This ethereal, delicious soup, with foie gras, chestnuts, and squab, is like a banquet in a single bite. I never ever tired of it, and because Jean-Louis was the model of consistency, his trademark soup tasted exactly the same, from the first time I ate it, to the very last, just a couple of months before his death. It remains simply the best soup I have ever tasted.

To simplify this soup, omit the quenelles, garnishing the soup instead with a slice of seared foie gras, if desired. An optional garnish that I like is a drizzle of reserved cooked foie fat. Use quail or duck breast instead of squab if you prefer.

SERVES 4

Chestnut–Foie Gras Soup

1 pound unpeeled chestnuts (scant 4 cups)
5 ounces fresh uncooked duck or goose foie gras (Grade C), trimmed and coarsely chopped
3 ounces lean prosciutto, chopped
¼ cup thinly sliced shallots
Freshly ground black pepper
3 cups chicken stock (page 8)
1½ cups heavy cream, more as needed
Fine sea salt

Squab Breast and Chestnut Quenelles

1 squab, dressed (about 12 ounces)
Fine sea salt and freshly ground black pepper
¼ cup plus 1 teaspoon heavy cream
1 teaspoon grapeseed oil
2 cups chicken stock (page 8)
1 ounce cooked duck meat, cut into ⅛-inch dice (about ¼ cup)

Garnish

4 tablespoons parsley chiffonade

PREPARE AN ICE BATH in a large bowl. To prepare the soup, bring 8 cups of water to a boil in a large saucepan. Add the chestnuts and blanch for 5 minutes. Drain immediately and transfer to the ice bath to cool. Drain the chestnuts again and slice off the bottom of each shell with a sharp knife; remove the entire shell. Mince 3 of the chestnuts and set aside for the quenelles. Set aside 10 more chestnuts for the garnish. Reserve the remaining chestnuts for the soup.

SET A HEAVY-BOTTOMED SAUCEPAN over high heat for 2 minutes. Add the foie gras and cook for about 1 minute, stirring occasionally. Add the chestnuts reserved for the soup, the prosciutto, and the shallots, and season generously with pepper. Stir together for 1 minute, add the chicken stock, and bring to a boil. Turn down the heat to a simmer and cook for 30 minutes, stirring and skimming occasionally. Transfer the mixture to a blender or food processor in batches and puree until smooth. Strain through a fine-mesh strainer into a clean heavy-bottomed saucepan, using the bottom of a ladle or a wooden spoon to force through as much liquid as possible (there should be a generous 2 cups of liquid). Stir in the cream, season with salt, and adjust the seasonings. Bring to a boil, stirring occasionally. Remove from the heat, let cool slightly, and refrigerate (the soup may be prepared several hours ahead).

TO PREPARE THE SQUAB BREAST, carve the breast meat from the carcass (save the carcass, if desired, for making stock). Trim away skin and any fat from the breast meat and chop ¼ cup of the meat; set aside. Finely dice the remaining breast meat into ⅛-inch cubes and set aside. Transfer the ¼ cup chopped squab breast meat into a food processor and season with salt and pepper. Process to a paste, add the cream, and continue processing just until well blended; do not overmix. Strain through a fine-mesh strainer into a small bowl, using the bottom of a ladle or a wooden spoon to force through as much of the mixture as possible (there should be about ⅓ cup of strained mixture). Stir in the 3 minced chestnuts, cover the bowl, and refrigerate.

SEASON THE FINELY DICED SQUAB BREAST MEAT with salt and pepper. Heat the oil in a small nonstick skillet set over high heat. When hot, add the squab and sauté for about 45 seconds, just until very lightly browned, stirring constantly. Drain on paper towels and chill in the refrigerator.

PREHEAT THE OVEN TO 250°F. About 15 minutes before serving, set a small nonstick skillet over high heat. Cut the 10 chestnuts reserved for garnish in half and add to the hot skillet. Roast for 6 to 8 minutes, until browned, turning occasionally. Transfer to a heatproof dish and set aside. About 5 minutes before you plan to serve, warm a soup tureen and four wide soup bowls in the oven.

MEANWHILE, FORM AND COOK THE QUENELLES. In a small skillet, bring the stock to a simmer and then remove from the heat. Using two teaspoons, mold the squab puree into oval shapes, allowing a scant 1 teaspoon of the mixture for each; you should have enough of the mixture to form 12 to 14 quenelles. Once formed, ease each quenelle into the hot stock. Once they are all formed, return the skillet to low heat, bring the stock to a gentle simmer, being careful not to boil, and let it cook for about 5 minutes, or until just cooked through. Set aside in the hot stock.

TO SERVE, REHEAT THE SOUP; if needed, thin with a little cream or some of the stock used for poaching the quenelles. Place the sautéed finely diced squab and the diced duck meat in the bottom of each warm soup bowl. Remove the quenelles from the stock with a slotted spoon and arrange 3 or 4 quenelles and the halved chestnuts reserved for garnish around the edge of the meat. Sprinkle each bowl with parsley chiffonade. Place the soup in the heated tureen for ladling into the bowls at the table.

Index

*Special thanks to the following for their generous
donations to this book's photo shoot:*

AHI BROTHERS SPECIALTY FISH
Ken Enomto
P.O. Box 1387
Pacifica, CA 94044
(415) 339-7483
www.ahibros.com

EXCLUSIVE FRESH, INC.
Phil Bruno
P.O. Box 308
El Granada, CA 94018
(650) 728-7321
www.exclusivefresh.com

GOLDEN GATE MEAT COMPANY
Frank Messmer
550 Seventh Street
San Francisco, CA 94103
(415) 861-3800
www.goldengatemeatcompany.com

GREENLEAF PRODUCE COMPANY
Paula Linton
1955 Jerrold Avenue
San Francisco, CA 94124
(415) 647-2991
www.greenleafsf.com

HERITAGE HOUSE, INC.
Leo Dreyer
2190 Palou Avenue
San Francisco, CA 94124
(415) 285-1331

PACIFIC PLAZA IMPORTS
Mark M. Bolourchi
2870 Howe Road #110
Martinez, CA 94553
(925) 335-9898
www.plazadecaviar.com

VERDURE FARMS
(HEIRLOOM TOMATO SPECIALISTS)
Tamara Scalera
2476 Westside Road
Healdsburg, California 95448
(707) 433-0194

VILLAGE IMPORTS/MADE IN
FRANCE
Cecily Costa
211 South Hill Drive
Brisbane, CA 94005
(415) 562-1120
www.levillage.com

VILLEROY & BOCH
Steve Marciel
www.villeroy-boch.com